THE BATTLE FOR ROOM 314

THE BATTLE FOR ROOM 314

My Year of Hope and Despair in
a New York City High School

ED BOLAND

GRAND CENTRAL
PUBLISHING

NEW YORK   BOSTON

Copyright © 2016 by Edward Boland

All rights reserved. In accordance with the U.S. Copyright Act of 1976, the scanning, uploading, and electronic sharing of any part of this book without the permission of the publisher constitute unlawful piracy and theft of the author's intellectual property. If you would like to use material from the book (other than for review purposes), prior written permission must be obtained by contacting the publisher at permissions@hbgusa.com. Thank you for your support of the author's rights.

Grand Central Publishing
Hachette Book Group
1290 Avenue of the Americas
New York, NY 10104

www.HachetteBookGroup.com

Printed in the United States of America

RRD-C

First Edition: February 2016

10 9 8 7 6 5 4 3 2 1

Grand Central Publishing is a division of Hachette Book Group, Inc.
The Grand Central Publishing name and logo is a trademark of Hachette Book Group, Inc.

The Hachette Speakers Bureau provides a wide range of authors for speaking events. To find out more, go to www.hachettespeakersbureau.com or call (866) 376-6591.

The publisher is not responsible for websites (or their content) that are not owned by the publisher.

Library of Congress Cataloging-in-Publication Data
Names: Boland, Ed, author.
Title: The battle for Room 314 : my year of hope and despair in a New York
   City high school / Ed Boland.
Description: First edition. | New York : Grand Central Publishing, 2016.
Identifiers: LCCN 2015032644| ISBN 9781455560615 (hardback) | ISBN
   9781478985327 (audio download) | ISBN 9781455560608 (ebook)
Subjects: LCSH: Boland, Ed. | High school teachers--New York (State)--New
   York--Biography. | Public schools--New York (State)--New York. |
   Education--New York (State)--New York. | BISAC: BIOGRAPHY & AUTOBIOGRAPHY
   / Educators.
Classification: LCC LA2317.B555 A3 2016 | DDC 373.11092--dc23 LC record available at
http://lccn.loc.gov/2015032644

ISBN 978-1-4555-6061-5

For Sam

Contents

Contents

"Education then, beyond all other devices of human origin, is the great equalizer of the conditions of men, the balance-wheel of the social machinery."

—*Horace Mann*

"In the midst of prosperity the mind is elated, and in prosperity a man forgets himself; in hardship he is forced to reflect on himself, even though he be unwilling."

—*Alfred the Great*

"I like to fight, I like to fuck, I like pie."

—*Merwin's ninth-grade "Getting To Know You" questionnaire*

THE BATTLE FOR ROOM 314

Chantay

CHANTAY MARTIN SAT on top of her desk, her back to me. A tight Old Navy T-shirt covered in rhinestones was riding up her thin brown back, exposing a baby-blue thong.

I leaned over and whispered firmly in her ear, "We had a deal, and you aren't holding up your end of it."

She yelled back, "What deal, mister?" in the kind of teenage voice that adults dread: belligerent, manic, almost painful at close range. She was chewing a wad of purple gum with such force and speed that she seemed to have a piston implanted in her jaw.

It was ten minutes before the three o'clock dismissal bell on a scorching hot September afternoon on the Lower East Side of Manhattan. A single oscillating fan strained to cool the classroom. Its white plastic head dutifully panned back and forth on Chantay, thirty other high school freshmen, and me, their anxious new teacher.

"Our deal was that you do your work and I won't call you out in public. 'No more drama,' remember?" I said in a desperate whisper, quoting a Mary J. Blige song—a pathetic attempt to find a sliver of common ground between a forty-three-year-old gay white guy from Chelsea and a teenage black girl from the projects of Bed-Stuy.

I was only five days into my new career as a ninth-grade history teacher, and precious little in the way of learning was getting done.

Chantay continued holding court with a group of her "gurlz," their chatter getting louder by the minute. The geography work sheets they were supposed to be completing were left untouched in a pile. At least the other groups of students had bothered to humor me by passing the papers out before ignoring them.

I shot Chantay a fierce look. She returned it with a light smile, as if she were on a talk show and had given the host an amusing answer. Our deal was clearly off, and I was angry, so I resorted to some old-school yelling: "Chantay, sit in your seat and get to work. *Now!*" I punched out the last word in what I thought was a strict teacher voice.

Crack! On the other side of the room, someone had hurled a calculator at the blackboard. My head snapped toward the trouble; it wasn't the only problem. A group of boys were shoving one another near a new laptop. Two girls swayed in sweet unison and mouthed lyrics while sharing the earphones of a strictly forbidden iPod. Another girl was splayed over her desk, lazily reading *Thug Luv 2* as if she were on a cruise

I heard Chantay's distinctive cackle again and turned back to her. She was now standing on top of her desk, towering above me like a pro wrestler on the ropes about to pounce. Her head was surrounded by a constellation of world currencies that hung from an economics mobile I had painstakingly constructed over the summer. I started to feel queasy and light-headed. No. It wasn't supposed to happen like this.

"Chantay, sit down immediately, or there will be serious consequences," I barked. All eyes were now darting back and forth between us like those of spectators at a tennis match.

She laughed and cocked her head up at the ceiling. Then she slid her hand down the outside of her jeans to her upper thigh, formed a long cylinder between her thumb and forefinger, and shook it. What the *hell* was she doing? She looked me right in the eye and screamed:

"SUCK MY FUCKIN' DICK, MISTER."

Stunned, I stood frozen in front of the class as it erupted. I didn't know a roomful of humans were capable of making that much noise. It sounded like a Hollywood laugh track times a hundred, a torrent of guffaws, lung-emptying laughs, and howls. Exhausted from laughter, the rabble paused and then:

"Oh no she *di'n't!*"

"Man, he can't even control the *girls.*"

Jesús, Chantay's badass boyfriend, glanced at her and grinned like an impresario, proud of the talent he had cultivated.

I'd always admired a filthy mouth, especially on a woman, and for a second I thought, *Touché, Miss Martin. If you have a dick, it is certainly bigger than mine. Well played. Very original.* Then I suddenly remembered that I was not in a bar talking smack with my friends. This was a classroom. I was her teacher. She was my student.

I yanked in a quick breath and frantically searched for a powerful, professional response. If I were to go apeshit, it would show that she'd really got to me. If I underreacted, I would appear passive and invite more trouble. But nothing came to me, nothing at all. I stood there paralyzed and afraid. My now-trembling legs were hidden inside my brand-new pair of Dockers. I was so unfamiliar with the feeling of fear that I barely recognized it.

In one fell swoop, Chantay fingered me not only as gay, but as her bitch, her power emanating from a penis she didn't have.

And, sadly, because it was a girl who'd staged this, it was viewed as an even greater humiliation for me. So much for the girls being the "easy ones" to control. Even the way she blocked the scene was strategic, with her towering on top of her desk while I circled helplessly below. The final touch was that she didn't even know my name. It wasn't worth remembering, just "mister" would suffice.

I should have simply walked out of the building, hailed a cab, and gone to the unemployment office. I had sunk the eight ball on the first break. Game over.

How had things gotten so bad, so quickly?

CHAPTER 1

The Good Ol' Days

JUST FOUR MONTHS earlier, eight sets of gilded, art deco doors suddenly crashed open and a sea of guests, the titans of Wall Street, flooded the ballroom of the Waldorf Astoria Hotel. I smoothed the lapels on my tuxedo, adjusted my headset, and took a deep breath. My staff and I had been working on this fund-raising event for almost a year, and still the inevitable last-minute crises came crackling over my earpiece:

"We're missing a floral arrangement on table 71. Someone contact Preston Tuttle immediately."

"Late seating change for the Teschner table. Lady Foster will now be seated between Mr. Teschner and Judge Sullivan. I repeat: Lady Foster goes to seat number one. Stat!"

"The tipsy associates at table 207 in the balcony have asked for a third bottle of wine and they haven't even sat down yet. Comply?"

"Negative."

"Bill Cunningham from the *Times* just arrived in the Jade Pavilion. He looks really grumpy. Where should I steer him?"

The final chimes sounded, the lights went down, and twelve hundred guests were seated in a collective *whoosh*. Blessedly, my worst fear—that people who had donated fifty thousand dollars for a table would find themselves without seats—didn't materialize; the two-day-long seating meeting had paid off. Ancient banquet waiters hobbled around the packed tables and indifferently slung paillards of chicken, limp asparagus, and oversalted risotto at the guests.

The evening's honoree, an extraordinarily generous hedge fund manager and near billionaire in his early forties, mounted the stage and announced from the podium that he was making a $1 million gift. He had already raised another million from his colleagues in the industry. All told, the event raised $4 million, a record for our organization. Project Advance finds the most promising minority kids from disadvantaged New York neighborhoods and prepares them to excel alongside the children of the ruling class at New York private schools and New England boarding schools. Before they are placed in their schools, the kids must complete a grueling fourteen-month academic boot camp over two summers and a school year. While their classmates are outside enjoying baseball, the beach, and *coco* ices, they are stuck inside every night with four hours of homework including Latin, *Great Expectations*, and algebra. Once they are in private school, the program offers them tremendous support and opportunities like internships at J.P. Morgan and MOMA, study abroad trips to Mongolia and Ghana, physics tutors, and a high-end SAT prep course.

By the end of their college careers, they have thoroughly Ivy pedigrees and are ready to change the world. The program has truly stellar results: More of its students earn degrees from Harvard than from any other university. But the individual stories of its alumni are even more compelling: The daughter of a poor immigrant from Chinatown won a Rhodes scholarship while at Harvard; a girl whose grandmother worked in the kitchen of the private girls' school she attended earned a full ride to Yale; and a Dominican kid who somehow managed to survive time in the city's homeless shelters became salutatorian at Princeton—and delivered his commencement address in Latin. The program's alumni roster boasts hundreds of lawyers and judges, surgeons and scientists, principals and professors. But they weren't just well-credentialed professionals, they remembered where they were from and they had an urgent desire to give back.

It had been a good run, a very good run, but I was feeling ready to move on to a new career. For five years I'd been the development director, responsible for raising the money for the program. It was gratifying to watch the kids soar at these private schools, at college, and beyond, but I also wanted to leave my administrative job, roll up my sleeves, and work directly with kids. I adored the organization and its mission, but I had a nagging feeling that the program, as worthy as it was, just wasn't reaching enough kids or the ones who needed the most help. Project Advance took only two hundred kids a year, but there were 1.1 million students in the New York City schools, more than the total population of San Francisco or Detroit. Wasn't there a way to help more of them get a decent education?

I'd started hatching a plan for a new career exactly two years before. In June of 2004, I was standing in the exact same spot at precisely the same time as the guests bolted out of the ballroom to their waiting town cars. I poured a glass of Bordeaux from an unfinished bottle at the chairman's table and caught up with one of the program's brightest stars, Sharon. Both brilliant and charismatic, she had just spent the dinner dazzling the chairman's guests with the ease of a debutante. With Project Advance's help, she had gone from a hardscrabble upbringing in the South Bronx to earn a full scholarship to Choate. She had thrived on its leafy campus, earned its top prize at graduation, and was now a sophomore at Harvard.

After regaling me with stories from Harvard Yard, she scanned the room. "This program made all the difference in my life. I'm grateful, but I also feel guilty. I just wish kids in public school could have the kinds of teachers and opportunities I had at Choate." She looked down and sighed. "But I guess the world doesn't work that way."

"You know, I've actually thought about teaching in the public schools. It's been a secret aspiration of mine for a long time," I confided in her. I had been mulling the idea for years but had told only my innermost circle.

"Really? In a public school?" Her face lit up. "You should do it. You're a natural. The kids will love you. How many times did all of you on staff repeat that quote to us: 'Education is the great equalizer'? You should go and teach. Try to level the playing field, at least a little." I felt a surge of adrenaline as she spoke.

For years I had been flirting with the idea of a second career in teaching. Right out of college, I had passed up an offer to teach at a Catholic high school in the Bronx, and I often wondered if I had missed my calling. Hearing those words of encouragement from Sharon, someone whose life had been so transformed by education, was the turning point.

Later that night in our Chelsea apartment, as I struggled to extract the cuff links from my ruffled tuxedo shirt, I told my boyfriend, Sam, that I had finally made up my mind to teach. I had met Sam, the unquestioned love of my life, in 1999 at tryouts for New York's gay volleyball league. His rocket-fast serve, dark good looks, and unfettered sense of creativity hooked me. On our first date we discovered we were both Geminis, as well as former bed wetters and English teachers in China. Seven years into the relationship, people still mistook us for a new couple in the infatuation stage.

Sam was his entirely supportive and loving self. "Of course you should do it. Yes, do it! Those kids need great teachers like you." He blessed my decision with a kiss.

But could our comfy bourgeois lives handle a huge cut in my salary? An independent filmmaker with little steady income, Sam had always joked that I was his "nonprofit sugar daddy." And at that point, Sam was desperately trying to raise money for his first feature-length project. That weekend we did the math, and we figured with a lot of sacrifices, we could make it work. No more cabs or cleaning lady; dump my shrink; bye-bye, dry cleaning. It wouldn't kill us to learn to use a bit of Fantastik, a capful of Woolite. Sam would add cater-waitering to his repertoire. I could work in the summers.

Next, I researched all the part-time master's programs in teaching in the city. I went to open houses, pored through course catalogs, and plotted out a plan that would have me in a classroom full-time in two years. I knew there were programs like Teach For America where I could start teaching sooner if I went to school at night while I taught during the day, but that seemed overwhelming and I didn't want to rush it.

About a month after the gala, I revealed my master plan to my family. My parents had traveled from upstate New York to visit my younger sister, Nora, in New Jersey. As we sat around her dining room table after supper, chatting and picking at what remained of a carrot cake, I shared the news. Predictably, Nora, a teacher in a state penitentiary, and my brother-in-law, Dan, a middle school science teacher, were thrilled. My older sister, Lynn, a therapist for the indigent, specializing in counseling wife beaters, addicts, and homeless people, cheered, "Another whore for the poor; welcome to the ranks."

We were Catholics to the core. Almost everyone in my extended family had been born in St. Mary's Catholic hospital, had endured parochial education all the way through college, and was destined to be buried in Holy Sepulchre Cemetery. My sisters and I, however, renounced Catholicism's righteousness and conservatism as adults. Nora became a Unitarian, Lynn joined a Catholic church so radical that she was excommunicated, and I ended up an atheist. But try as we might, we couldn't really escape it, couldn't scrub the do-gooder scent off of ourselves, and we each ended up in some version of a helping profession.

I knew my father would be on board with my decision, too. He not only treasured education but was always a champion of the underserved. When we were kids, he would come home after his night shift at the Xerox plant and, despite our wailing, recite Dylan Thomas poetry, quote Saint Thomas Aquinas, and re-create dramatic passages of the *Decline and Fall of the Roman Empire*, making us play the roles of different barbarians at the gates of the Eternal City.

They all congratulated me with raised glasses and wished me luck. All eyes were now on my mother. I knew she would be a much tougher sell. You might imagine that such a ferocious Catholic, a woman who attended Mass daily, who volunteered endlessly at different charities, would welcome my turn to service. Weren't we the family that had spent some Thanksgiving nights at a homeless shelter in a church basement? You would think that she would be most proud of her daughters, who were in the trenches, doing "God's work." But no. It was an open secret that my mother's first loves were glamour and celebrity. Jesus was a close third.

She even infused glamour into her part-time job, a poodle grooming business she operated out of our basement. Every pooch, from tiny toy poodles to huge standard ones, would prance out of our basement with painted toenails, a spritz of Jean Naté perfume, and a crowning topknot adorned with a red bow.

When she went to the Most Precious Blood Church hospice "to help people die," in her words, she did her overnight bedside vigils in full makeup and wearing her good jewelry. She carried a sack of reading material that included *Architectural Digest*, *W*, the *New York Post* dog-eared to Page Six, and the *National Enquirer* to see her through the long volunteer shift. Deep down, she always loved the fact that in my career as a fund-raiser, I rubbed shoulders with the upper crust of New York.

Over the years, when I was home for the holidays I would hear little snippets of her conversations with friends on the phone, in which she would exaggerate my proximity to celebrity: "Beverly Sills shared her secret stash of Girl Scout cookies with Eddie at their meeting last week. I think they were the Lemon Cremes." "Did you know the dining room in the mayor's mansion has a custom-colored lighting system? Eddie told me." "Of course he knows Phil Donahue. Marlo, too!"

That night, thanks to a hefty infusion of her favorite Ernest and Julio Gallo rotgut red wine, her reaction to my announcement about being a public school teacher was even more unfiltered than usual.

"You are going to do *what?*" The alarm in her voice was clear and growing. "You're telling me you are going to take an eighty-thousand-dollar pay cut to teach in a *public* school? You have a wonderful job and you are already helping those smart, poor kids. Jesus, isn't that enough?"

"This is important to me. I need to try it," I told her calmly.

She narrowed her eyes and exaggerated an exhale. "Oh, go on then, be a teacher, *BE A LOSER!*"

I glanced across the table at my sister and brother-in-law, the two teachers. By now, we were all used to this kind of outrageous remark, which had tumbled out of her mouth at the most awkward times throughout our lives. Yet, everyone—from closest family to complete strangers—seemed to tolerate and forgive my mother's transgressions. I've never known why. Was it her tone of impunity?

The hint of *Town & Country* glamour she brought to our blue-collar neighborhood? Or was it that she quickly reverted to kindness and compliments after insulting people?

My father, David, known widely as Saint Joseph for his good works and selfless disposition, delivered his predictable but toothless reprimand: "Jesus, Julie! Would you please watch what you say?"

I looked to my sister and brother-in-law to make sure they hadn't taken it to heart, and then we all broke into laughter. My mother realized her gaffe, smiled sheepishly, and patted the braided bun she was famous for. My sister Nora came over and rubbed my shoulders. "You are welcome to come to this loser's classroom any time you want to see what you are getting yourself into."

"What the fuck you doin' here?"

A young criminal from southern New Jersey growled at me as he leaned his skinny frame down to the desk I was sitting in. His face was far closer to mine than I wanted. Even though my sister Nora was only fifteen feet away writing something on the blackboard and a security guard was sitting in the hall, I was a bit shaken up. A small band of tousled and rowdy-looking teenage boys wearing baggy orange jumpsuits filed into the classroom, their heads jerking with hip-hop swagger.

"Boys, take out your phonics work sheet, the one about the long and short *u*," my sister gently commanded.

As soon as she turned around the kid quickly retreated to the other side of the room. Maybe he wasn't so tough after all. I exhaled. A petite, pale ash blonde in her late thirties, my sister looked wildly out of place in a men's jail, but she acted like she owned the place.

"Kelvin, don't even think of sitting near Marco. We all know that is a bad idea." She spoke firmly but respectfully to her charges.

I scanned the room. I expected prison school to look seriously grim, but in truth it was no more cinder-block, fluorescent-light ugly than most public schools.

"We have an observer today. Mr. Boland. Please welcome him," she said.

"Looks like her brother," said the boy who had "greeted" me.

"Yo, is that your brother, miss?"

"It's her bro, man."

"Brother, no doubt."

Either she chose to ignore the astute comments or the hearing aid she wore didn't pick them up. Our family often joked that being oblivious to what her students said was the secret to her teaching success.

I had come to learn at her feet. If I was going to make a midlife transition to being an urban high school teacher, there was no one better to learn from than Nora. In her fifteen years of teaching, she had seen it all: First, in a parochial school in Maryland, a monsignor had molested one of her students. Next, she taught in a Special Education classroom in a different Maryland high school that served as a catchall for outcasts: kids with muscular dystrophy, pregnant girls, generic delinquents, and a student named Bobbie—a giant boy with Down syndrome who relieved his anxiety on the daily bus ride home by pulsing his considerable behind against the window. (One particularly stressful day, he shattered the back window with it, bringing traffic to a complete halt.) Even that wasn't enough of a challenge for Nora, so she then applied to teach in this state juvenile penitentiary. During her interview, she had sealed the deal with a line I later parroted for my own job interviews: "The reluctant learner is my specialty."

And reluctant they were. For most of these boys, this was their fifth or sixth attempt to learn to read. I tried not to cringe as I watched sixteen-year-olds struggle to pronounce the simplest words. They looked both pained and eager, contorting their mouths like tropical fish lunging toward flakes of food.

"Remember, it's *a*, like *apple*, sounds like *ahhh*. Say it with me: *A*, *apple*, *ahhh*." She gently coached and coaxed them.

They mocked one another horribly. "Yeah, nigga, didn't you hear her? Say it with me: *D, duh, dumb ass*. You a dumb ass, son."

But overall I was struck by how well-behaved most of them were. Later, at lunch, she told me just how much power she wielded. "They don't get too out of hand. One word from me to the principal and they are denied use of the canteen, lose visitor privileges, or, worst of all, they're stripped of their sneakers for a month and put in paper shoes. Nobody wants that." I listened raptly.

"But don't worry, they get plenty out of hand sometimes. Yesterday, somebody yelled out, 'Miss, you got a little chalk in your mustache.' And last week, one kid asked his buddy out loud, 'Hey, how old do you think Miss is?' And the other little punk said, 'Hard to tell, 'cause she got zits *and* wrinkles.'" She laughed. "Can you believe the shit they say? I'm glad I can't hear a lot of it."

Nora was always and forever the champion of the underdog. She was a textbook good girl as a kid, always bringing home a parade of nearly dead animals, in cardboard boxes, on Frisbees, in her bare hands—only to watch them die on our dining room table soon after. In fifth grade, she babysat for free for some poor kids whose mother worked long hours. She spent college summers volunteering in places like Malawi and India. But make no mistake, my sister was no sappy savior. Nora's compassion was always clear-eyed and tough. In fact, when she went to Calcutta to work in an orphanage, she joined forces not with Mother Teresa, but rather with the good sister's secular rival, Dr. Jack, a drunken Englishman who did the same good work but refrained from proselytizing. And as an adult, she and her husband, a surfer she'd talked out of law school and into teaching, raised four amazing children (two of them adopted from neglectful homes) and one terribly behaved dog, Tigger, who ate everything from boxes of Brillo pads to her used tampons.

As Nora made her way from desk to desk, I tried inconspicuously to scan the boys' faces, imagining their crimes, their futures, and the lousy hands they had been dealt in the first place. Just standing by the copy machine before class, I heard other teachers make reference to an arsonist, a drug kingpin, and a foot fetishist who hid underneath dress racks in department stores waiting to lick the toes of unsuspecting women. I knew they had done horrible things, but they didn't look particularly fearsome—except for one boy, Mario. The minute he walked in the door he fixed me with a wild-eyed "Who the fuck you lookin' at?" stare. He had a prison-yard physique, a towering power-fro, and an elaborate neck tattoo. He caught me trying to decipher its interlocking Italianate letters and he fixed me again with a steely look that made me hold my breath. I reprimanded myself silently: *Man up. It's gonna be a lot worse than this when you are teaching on your own in Bed-Stuy.*

During silent reading time, Nora and I stood in the doorway. I covered my mouth and said, "Mario's tattoo is sure eye-catching. Are those his initials? M.O.B.?"

"Oh no, silly, it's his gang, 'Money Over Bitches.' Can you believe that name? I think he is high up in their 'administration.'" She looked at her watch and sighed, "M.O.B. Well, at least they're clear about their priorities."

Toward the end of class, Nora announced, "Boys, it's time for a read aloud." I thought it seemed babyish, but they were game. She read a short story about a suburban middle school girl who was ashamed of her ailing Indian grandfather who had come to live with her family. In reading the final paragraphs, she slowed down notice-ably. I figured she was getting bored or had detected some trouble at the back of the room, but it soon became clear that the story's sad ending moved her when the grandfather died. Her voice tightened and her eyes welled up. My brotherly urge to protect her swelled. *Is she crazy? She can't show vulnerability in front of these kids. They'll eat her for lunch!*

I looked around the room. Most of the boys had their heads down or were staring blankly forward, seeming not to register the story or my sister's reaction. And then I saw Mario, who'd locked eyes with my sister.

"Yo, miss, that really hit you, huh?" He said it again, more slowly: "Really hit you." He made a fist, thumped his heart, and softly extended his arm to her in a gentle salute.

The moment touched me deeply. Where I thought she had made the worst mistake, she showed her mastery. She made herself vulnerable, and the toughest kid in the room had responded in kind. It was the last place on earth I would have expected such a tender, human exchange. I was covered with chills.

A buzzer rang and the boys scrambled madly for the door.

I walked through the prison parking lot exhilarated. Nora had shown me the good stuff. Even the toughest kid could be reached. If I could be a quarter as good as she was, it would be tremendously fulfilling. I'd had enough of Project Advance's safe haven. The front lines of education called. I wanted in.

Chapter 2

Best Practices

For two years, I had poured my heart into my graduate education courses at City University, all the while working full-time at Project Advance. I got used to late-night study jags in the library and had to give up most weekends writing papers and reading. I was determined to make it work. But now it was time to put away the books, hit the trenches, and plunge into student teaching. To become certified as a teacher, New York State required two placements over five months, one in middle school and one in high school. As excited as I was about gaining the experience, it meant that I had to give up my job (and my income) but still pay tuition for the privilege of working full-time for free. Ouch! I had saved a nest egg for these months and Sam and I had a serious austerity plan in place, but I wondered how others managed to afford to live during this apprentice period.

I was frankly not too enthused about the middle school requirement. Teaching history at that level seemed so basic and literal. Goofy textbooks with cartoon characters acting out the American Revolution made me roll my eyes. And more important, that age of student just wasn't intriguing to me. As so many of us were at that age, the students were stuck in an awkward phase—no longer baby-fat, grade school cute, but developing acne and body odor on ungainly frames. You could practically watch as they were deciding between the tug of naughty adolescence and childhood innocence. I thought I would prefer the wit and brio of high schoolers.

My first assignment was at Yorkville Heights School, a public middle school right on the border of Harlem and the Upper East Side of Manhattan. On paper, it was an impressive place, boasting solid scores and an enviable placement record at the city's better high schools, but still serving a diverse and largely poor population. Three-quarters of the students qualified for free lunch, the benchmark of poverty or near poverty.

Even before I set foot in the place, I could see why the school got results. The principal, Evette Russo, stood on East Ninety-Seventh Street in a Hillary-esque pantsuit greeting families, directing buses, and giving the stink-eye to a bunch of thuggy-looking teenagers on the corner. Friendly but all-business, she pegged me even before I stepped foot in the school: "You must be the new student teacher." Seeing I was no kid, she said, "A career changer, eh? That's good. And we're happy to have another man here. The boys need more male role models." Without taking her eyes off all the bedlam, she pointed back toward a bank of windows. "You'll be with Lindsay Wells, sixth grade, in room 306. She's a literacy whiz. You'll learn everything you need to know from her."

Room 306, to my naive eye, seemed close to an educational paradise. The room was as neat as a pin, but somehow at the same time was bursting with books, art supplies, mobiles, computer stations, plants, and a hamster whirring on an exercise wheel. Carefully decorated bulletin boards packed with student work alternated with corny inspirational posters that said things like "Why fit in when you were born to stand out?" or "If you expect respect, be the first to show it."

The room felt bustling and lively, but not in a chaotic way. Some kids were reading quietly, a few were on computers, and others socialized in little clusters. They were remarkably diverse, not only in terms of race and ethnicity but also in terms of development. Many of the girls looked mature enough to have been in eighth or even ninth grade; some were experimenting with makeup and adult jewelry, while others were still happy to be covered in the primary colors of grammar school and kid jewelry they probably got as a favor at a birthday party. Most of the girls towered over the boys, many of whom still looked like adorable, round-faced fourth or fifth graders.

Ms. Wells, who was in her late twenties and had the theatrical good looks of Bettie Page, stood up from her desk. As soon as the clock hit 8:30, she gave a rapid series of syncopated handclaps. Like an echoed birdcall, every student, without hesitation, repeated the clap sequence back to her and then the room fell completely silent. It was cultish, Pavlovian, and deeply impressive. With a reaction like that from the kids, I expected her to be a sour martinet, but she was cheery and sweet. Without saying a word, she gave me a quick and knowing adult-to-adult smile. Many of the kids looked at me and whispered, but she put a stop to that simply by saying, "Eyes on me." They complied.

I sat down and observed. In the next ninety minutes, she read a short story aloud, gave a mini-lesson on adverbs, collected field-trip fees, fixed a computer, and applied a Band-Aid (the last two seemingly at the same time). In the final minutes of the period, she detected some well-concealed skulduggery involving three boys, some crumpled singles, and a basketball pool. What couldn't she do? At the end of class, she introduced me to the students, who eyed me warily. Afterward she said, "Don't worry, they'll get used to you."

Over lunch I sat down with the whole sixth-grade team, as diverse in appearance as temperament: Ruthie, the assertive and whip-smart black chick with a confectionary updo of thick braids; Joel, the nebbishy and shy Jewish guy with chunky glasses and a penchant for curriculum; and Lindsay, the long-haired and vivacious white girl, who would have looked at home on a milking stool on a Midwestern farm. From the way they talked to one another, you could tell they had worked together for years. They were welcoming and helpful, but I also got the sense they were a tiny bit fatigued at the ongoing cycle of overeager and clueless student teachers coming through the door.

The next afternoon, while leading the after-school dance club in a rousing reggaeton number, Lindsay tripped on a backpack and rolled her ankle. In the frenzy of the dance, the kids didn't seem to notice, so I went over to help her. As I pulled her up, she muttered under her breath, "Damn it, I have a show tonight at the Slipper Room." She winced in pain.

"That strip joint?" I said without thinking.

"It's burlesque, not stripping," she replied evenly, without a hint of apology. I tried not to act surprised. It wasn't easy. Literacy expert by day, burlesque artist by night.

"Of course, I understand. It's very different." I was eager to show her I was no square.

After I sent a kid to the nurse's office for an ice pack, I was helping Ms. Wells elevate the ankle on her desk when she said, "You should come see a show sometime. My stage name is Rocky Bottom." What were the other teachers up to in their spare time? I wished I had such an exciting double life.

Over the next six weeks, I watched Ms. Wells guide her sixth-grade charges adroitly, keeping them focused on learning even though they were in the throes of early puberty and social treachery. She helped me plan the social studies lessons I was charged with teaching and gave me great feedback: "This graphic would be better presented as a Venn diagram...You'll never cover all that material in a forty-five-minute period...This website is written at a ninth-grade level." While I am sure it was occasionally helpful for her to have another adult in the room, I was, on balance, just a whole lot more work for her—one more needy student but older, bigger, and with ten times the number of questions. Over dinner every night, I bored Sam with tales of my Jamestown Colony lesson and the ever-shifting alliances I observed among the girls. The social drama of middle school was unchanged, even from my day.

One afternoon during a vocabulary quiz, I caught Ricardo blatantly copying off the paper of his neighbor Jaquan. I was surprised to see it from such a sweet and timid kid. Ricardo had been held back and was older and taller than his classmates. He was beanpole thin, nothing but elbows, knees, and ears. I confiscated both papers and walked them over to Ms. Wells, explaining the situation, hoping to be praised for my vigilance. I told her I thought we should read Ricardo the riot act after school.

Lindsay narrowed her eyes. "Before we scold him, let's try to understand his motivation. I suspect Ricardo was cheating because he couldn't do the work, not because he didn't want to do the work." I nodded, a little embarrassed. I had retained more of the disciplinary trappings of my parochial school past than I cared to admit. I reminded myself that Ricardo was learning-disabled and struggled to keep up in almost every subject. "Use this as a teachable moment. Of course, we'll tell him what he did was wrong, but let's give him the opportunity to learn it on his own and show us he can do it. Save the lecture for later." It was such humane and wise advice. I was humbled, particularly since, until recently, I was normally the one giving professional advice to twenty-somethings like Lindsay who worked for me.

At her direction, I helped Ricardo create some vocabulary flash cards after school that day. We went over them until I was practically dizzy, but he kept getting them wrong. Frustrated, I found myself using more complicated words to explain simpler ones.

"Col·lab·o·rate," he read the card slowly.

"You know, it's like pooling resources," I said.

"Like swimming?"

"Swimming?"

"You said pool."

"No, not like swimming; it's a different kind of pool. I should have said 'work together.'"

It was hard for me to get out of my overeducated head and break things down for him. This kind of patience didn't come naturally to me. The next day, Ricardo scraped by on the quiz with a 6 out of 10. I rated myself a 4 out of 10 in helping him. Lesson learned: Stern lectures are fast and easy; teaching material to a struggling kid is long and hard. And this was only one small quiz. Would there be enough support along the way to help this boy get to high school graduation?

My time at the middle school culminated in a "publishing party." Over the course of a month, every kid had read several books around a theme (playing to type, almost invariably sports figures for boys and distressed animals or bold heroines for girls) and then wrote a book report about their favorite one. Ms. Wells and I went through several rounds of revisions with each of the students. It was so easy to see what was wrong in their writing, but so terribly hard to explain how to fix it. Simply correcting them wasn't enough.

The day of the party arrived. Outside "experts" (parents, friends of teachers, other faculty members) were brought in to read the final reports and hear short presentations from the authors. The visiting adults wrote thoughtful evaluations and so did the other students. Lindsay told me, "The trick is that even the most un-motivated kid cares if she has to present her work to outsiders.

Everybody works harder for an audience. I should know." She winked at me.

Ricardo had struggled to fill a full page about a picture book on Jackie Robinson, but his effort was obvious. Drita, a star student who arrived only a few years before from Macedonia, presented a five-page essay on a hefty Helen Keller biography, complete with footnotes. As I panned the room, watching the students present in serious and scholarly tones, I got chills. I promised myself then that I would do all I could to make my classroom look and feel just like this when I was at the helm in the fall.

On my last day at Yorkville Heights, I pulled open the window and looked down at the kids as they rushed onto the street at dismissal time. Like a toss of confetti, they spread in every direction in a burst of brightly colored coats and backpacks. After a few minutes they were all gone, and the sidewalk returned to its drab, gum-mottled gray. As I'd been during my visit to Nora's classroom, I was inspired as well as intimidated by the experience. Nora and Lindsay made it look so easy; but I knew it was anything but. I hoped I had the stuff they did.

Saying good-bye to Ms. Wells, I choked up. "I admire everything that you're doing here. I've learned so much. I hope I can put it into practice. Thank you."

She gave me a hug. "You clearly have the knack for teaching. You're going to be a star, I just know it."

On a gray morning the next week, my fellow student teacher Gabe Marwell and I stood on the Park Avenue sidewalk peering up at a skyscraper, incredulous that there was a high school inside. The Eugene Debs High School for Business Careers was a sagging bundle of contradictions. It was located on Park Avenue, but nothing about it called to mind that opulent address. Hidden in the lower floors of an ugly skyscraper that housed some Fortune 500 companies higher up, it drew its students from the poorest outer-borough neighborhoods. Although the school was named for America's leading socialist, its purported mission was to foster young captains of capitalism. It appeared to be a school, yet it looked, functioned, and smelled like a penitentiary, bursting with more than three thousand students.

A little Internet research had given me some insight into the place before I started. A full-blown riot the year before had led the police to establish a "mini-precinct" inside the school. Tabloid articles warned of "dangerous overcrowding" and a dropout rate hovering around 50 percent. As if all that wasn't damning enough, a chirpy online "review" from a recent graduate declared: "this is a grate school. awsome buziness programs!!!"

Gabe and I had become friendly in grad school. Like me, he was a forty-something career changer who had given up corporate accounting to give teaching a go. He was exactly what the system needed. He not only had a superb command of history, but he was a black man in a school system that had far too few role models for its young men of color to identify with.

For all its badass reputation, the school was eerily quiet when we entered. The security guard barely looked up from his *New York Post* before waving us past the metal detector and bag scanner. What a grim place. Every surface was covered in a color that defied a name, somewhere between shit brown and dyspeptic orange. Escalators covered in chain-link fencing connected its ten floors, thumping ominously in the silence. Lining the walls were posters printed in grayish block letters; even cheery events ("Spirit Week!") and felicitous messages ("Congratulations Boys Basketball Team!") looked like Stalinist pronouncements.

We made our way to the main office, where a tired-looking secretary slowly wheeled herself over to us on a creaking desk chair to which she seemed permanently attached. We explained that we were reporting for duty.

She turned her lizardy eyes up at us through a pair of bifocals. "You might have noticed there are no students for you to student-teach today. Why did they send you now? It's nothing but faculty meetings all day long." She exhaled for a long time, and then said, "Go see the history department head on the ninth floor."

We packed into a crowded but silent elevator filled with casually dressed teachers.

"Good morning, gentlemen, and just who are you going to see today, all dressed up so nice like that?" came a disembodied voice with a heavy Long Island accent from the back of the elevator. I was starting to miss the friendly sixth-grade Mod Squad at Yorkville Heights.

"Mr. Frank in Social Studies," I responded, tugging self-consciously at my tie.

"Oh, well, if you're gonna go see Humpty Dumpty, you better bring 'im a doughnut. That one, he sure likes his doughnuts." Some teachers openly laughed; others tried to conceal their widening smiles.

We excused our way out of the elevator; its heavy doors clacked shut behind us. I mumbled to Gabe, "If that's how the faculty acts, what are the kids going to be like?" He shrugged.

We walked into Mr. Frank's office. There sat a nearly round, balding, middle-aged white man. He wore an eggshell-white shirt that matched his skin tone exactly. The teachers in the elevator were mean but correct; he had a hint of powdered sugar left over on his cheek. His office was in utter disarray, crammed with overflowing army-green file cabinets.

He had obviously not been expecting company and jumped to

his feet. "They told you to come *today?*" He started flipping quickly through a black plastic binder, seeming eager to get rid of us. "Let's see. Are you Boland? You will be assigned to, ummm, Mr., ummm, Mr. Cooper. His first class is tomorrow at 7:15 in room 811. We are way, way overenrolled here, so classes go in shifts from 7:00 a.m. to almost 5:00 p.m. It's a bilingual economics class. And, uh, Marwell, you'll be with Miss Lewis."

"Unfortunately, I don't speak much Spanish," I confessed.

"Neither does Mr. Cooper. Oh, and let me find you the key to the faculty bathroom." Gabe and I exchanged wary glances as he dug through mounds of paper looking for the key. "That's all you really need to know for now."

The next morning at 6:55 a.m., my hair still wet from the shower, I walked past long lines of students undergoing the degrading daily metal-detector search. Outside the classroom, a few bleary-eyed kids were milling around. They kept trying the door and then half-heartedly kicking it. They eyed me suspiciously. I introduced myself to a few of them in Spanish with a smile and a handshake. Conversation was tough with the limits of my *Sesame Street* Spanish, but I learned that most of them had been up since 5:00 a.m. and had spent more than an hour on the subway to get there.

In the distance, I heard some faint shouting. It became louder and angrier as it got closer. This wasn't just some boisterous kids. It sounded violent.

Jesus, really? Already? Even trouble starts early here.

I walked briskly down the hall to the security station. Empty. The shouting grew closer. I'd be damned if I was going to break up a fight in my first hour there, but I thought I should at least see what was going on.

I rounded the hall, trailed by a few curious kids. Near the elevators stood two grown men, screaming at the top of their lungs, their faces inches from each other. In unison, they stopped and looked at me. I looked at the floor. The kids laughed.

A mustached, fiftyish black man with the sad eyes of Richard Pryor walked toward me. He wore a cheap suit and carried a beat-up brown plastic briefcase. He disdainfully threw one last comment over his shoulder: "You are very unprofessional, Dr. Cortona."

His far-taller opponent had a perfectly coiffed head of salt-and-pepper hair and a slightly less cheap suit. Still panting, he shot back in a heavy accent that was half Italian, half Count Chocula, "And I don't-a respect you, Meester Cooo-per."

"Are you the new student teacher?" Mr. Cooper asked as he approached me.

"Yes. Ed Boland." I squeezed out a smile.

"I'm, ahh, sorry you had to witness that. We were having a...professional disagreement." He looked down, shamefaced. This was the "master teacher" I was supposed to be learning from?

"I see" was all I could offer as we walked toward his classroom with the entire class in tow, tittering and commenting in Spanish behind us. He unlocked the classroom door and pushed it open with his shoulder.

Mr. Cooper announced that since it was the first day of a new quarter and many of the students were new, they must fill out a small yellow index card with their name, phone number, and address. Then he said the students could talk quietly for the remaining fifty minutes of the period. A Spanish translator who had trailed in a little late delivered a couple of rapid-fire sentences to the students about the index cards and then retired to the back of the room to pay a stack of bills. Cooper sat down at his desk, opened his briefcase, and unsuccessfully tried concealing the *Daily News* sports section behind it. He repeated the same routine for every one of his five periods that day. He said hardly a word to me.

A free day could be forgiven under many circumstances, but it didn't take much to figure out that eight months into the school year, there had been many such days. These kids didn't know jack about economics. In the next class, European History, I asked a thin, quiet girl with her head on her desk if I could glance at her notebook. It dutifully noted the date and topic of every class, but was filled with just a few simple phrases: "Reasons for WWI: bad economy, alliances. Results of WWI: punish Germany."

I wandered the room. An unclaimed report titled "Puerto Rico" sat curled in a wire bin in the corner. An odd topic for a European history class, I thought. I flipped through three typed pages of garbled sentence fragments surrounded by fat margins; the final page was nothing but a tourist map of the island pasted from the Internet, featuring a smiling sun sporting a straw hat, shades, and a cocktail. This level of work wouldn't even cut it in elementary school in the suburbs. Here it earned the kid a B. Mr. Cooper's sole comment was "Nice job."

I scanned the room, noting its ready cliques and clear racial fissures. Black kids to the left, Latinos to the right, a trio of Asians near the radiator. There was not a single white student in any of Mr. Cooper's classes. (As a matter of fact, the only white student in the entire ninth grade of eight hundred students was the son of some fairly prominent Eastern European UN diplomats who were probably clueless about the school's violent reputation.)

As I watched class after class come and go, it didn't seem that high school had changed that much since I was sixteen, but a closer inspection showed just how different things were: Three baby-faced sophomore boys conversed in a cluster of desks ahead of me. I shamelessly eavesdropped and they didn't hold back.

The smallest boy was very agitated. "Man, those phone sex lines are a whole lot of bullshit. I'm looking for free tail and they full of hookers. They think I'm gonna pay two bucks a minute to find a two-hundred-dollar ho?" His indignity was so convincing I practically found myself nodding in assent. I had to remind myself not to be amused. The closest transgression my friends and I had committed in ninth-grade Catholic school was when we were overheard by a priest as we tried to translate "blow job" into Latin.

On the other side of the room, a ring of Dominican girls were getting rowdy. They all wore necklaces that spelled out their names in cursive gold letters: Mariselleta, Jalisane, and Regaline. They were a striking bunch, particularly in profile, with gelled jet-black ringlets pressed against their temples. Their ringleader had her back to me, but I could hear her holding court. She turned her head a quarter and I realized it was a boy. He snapped, he quipped, he tossed his sassy head. A Latino Liberace was flaming about the room, and nobody seemed to give a shit. I sat awestruck. In my day, even a hint of girliness would get you bullied. To say Javan was unapologetically gay was an understatement. Here, if anything, he was bullying the straight boys, leading withering group assessments of boys' physiques. "Yes, girl, he do have booty, but, let's see, is he packin' up front? Don't think so!"

The rich characters and sensory overload made for a surreal experience, a stark contrast to any other first day of work I'd ever had. At the colleges and nonprofits where I had worked, I was always greeted by smiling professionals saying things like "You are going to love it here...Nice tie...Lunch is on us today." Most of my days at Project Advance were spent at the headquarters in a brownstone on the Upper West Side quietly tapping out e-mails or attending meetings with well-mannered overachievers. I didn't quite know whom to be more surprised by, the students who were so unabashed in their naughty ways or the ineffectual adults who were supposed to be educating them. Good-bye, fountains, statues, and quads. Hello, metal detectors, brown-bag lunches, and nearly brawling coworkers.

I pedaled my bike home through midtown traffic eager to share every last mad detail with Sam. In preparation for casting his upcoming movie, he was at our kitchen table, sorting through a mountain of headshots from smiling actors, when I got home. I was so wound up I didn't even take off my coat for the first hour as I told him story after story. After a while, he reached across the table and put his hand on top of mine. "Well, baby, it sounds like a real shit show, but if anyone is up to the challenge, you are. But maybe you should think about teaching in middle school." Pumped full of adrenaline from the day's events, I could barely sleep that night.

The next day during European History class, Mr. Cooper took attendance for a full ten minutes, bumbling over and butchering every last Asian and Latino name, save Chin and Perez. "Today, we start World War II," he announced in a voice that sounded deceptively like that of a teacher.

He was immediately interrupted: "Hey mister, I heard Hitler was a faggot."

The avalanche started.

"Yeah. I heard he was a Jew."

"One ball in his sack, that's all that bad boy had was one motherfuckin' ball. My uncle told me," said Javan, the Latino Liberace.

"Eww, gross," squealed a pair of girls in unison.

"Silence!" Mr. Cooper bellowed to no avail and a wave of chuckles. "Copy these notes." He alluded to the blackboard full of seemingly unrelated facts about the war (the terms "inflation economy" and "Kalashnikov rifle" were close to each other). Soon the room was thick with sighs of boredom. I remembered the same mindless transcription of notes from my own high school Social

Studies class. It seemed almost calculated to make the kids hate history, and it made me angry.

Fifteen minutes later, in the middle of a lecture and apropos of nothing, Cooper held up the B&H Photo catalog, a monster compendium of cameras and photography supplies, as if it were a bible. "Did you know there are cameras in here that cost four thousand dollars?" he asked the class, with the first hint of enthusiasm he'd shown all day. He cited their shutter speeds and telescopic ranges. A chubby girl in oversize glasses rolled her eyes at me. "Oh mister, please, not *that* thing again." She turned to me. "This is supposed to be a social studies class."

Could all the teachers here be this bad? I thought to myself as I rode the escalator down to the teachers' lounge. I was happy to find Gabe there. In hushed tones, he described his mentor-teacher, the earth mother Ms. Lewis, as burned out and boring, but his experience hardly seemed like the educational malpractice Mr. Cooper was committing five times daily. I tried to explain how dire it was.

"Come on, Ed. You don't need to exaggerate. You're quite entertaining enough," he chided me.

"Oh yeah, Mr. CPA, don't believe me? I dare you to observe Cooper's econ class later this week with me."

"Deal."

That Friday, I introduced Gabe to Mr. Cooper before the start of class. I fibbed and said Gabe was eager to observe Econ since he was probably going to be teaching it the next year. Before class, we stood around making small talk.

"Can I ask you guys a personal question?" Mr. Cooper asked.

"Please do," Gabe chirped. I cringed. During a little chat the day before, Cooper had asked me if the rumor that I was a "real homosexual" was true. I'd confirmed it with a smile.

What did he want to know now? "I heard you guys are both taking serious pay cuts to go into teaching," he said.

Gabe said yes. I nodded.

"Why would you ever do that?" Cooper continued, incredulous. I couldn't believe he was serious.

Gabe fielded this one: "I think every kid is entitled to have good teachers, particularly disadvantaged kids like these. I would like to be one of those teachers someday."

"Really?" Cooper was still mystified.

Gabe and I both settled in at the back of the room. At the front, Cooper had scribbled definitions of *asset* and *liability* on the board, which most of the awake students were jotting down. He gave them most of the class time to copy down those definitions and some screwy graphs. Then he launched into a short lecture about the material with a sense of conviction I hadn't yet seen in him. "An asset can appreciate or depreciate in value," he explained. "For example, a car appreciates in value over time; you can sell it for more than you paid. It's useful *and* it's an investment."

Gabe, normally a sedate kind of guy, suddenly looked like he'd just eaten something extraordinarily hot—wide-eyed, panicked, urgent. I shot him my best "You see?!" look. He seemed about to burst.

After class, in the hallway, he couldn't contain himself. "That's so unfair. It's hard enough for these kids to get this stuff right, even when you explain it clearly. But to steer them so wrong—it's criminal. My God, a car is the textbook definition of asset depreciation!"

Descending the escalators at the end of the day, we discussed ways to right the wrong, but it seemed so futile. Who to tell? What to say? We were powerless little cogs in the machine. Not only was Cooper disheartening to watch, but I resented that I was paying tuition to watch his daily fiasco. I planned my escape. After a faculty meeting the next week, I bold-facedly lied to Mr. Cooper and the department chair, Mr. Frank, saying I had a job offer for next year that was contingent on my having student-taught American History, and that I needed to be assigned to a new classroom.

I started shopping around for a new master teacher. It was slim pickings. After I had observed just about every other teacher in the history department, I settled on my target: Ruth Wasserman, a fiery, petite, redheaded veteran in her fifties. She ran a pretty tight ship, assigned homework, and appeared to know what she was talking about. I repeated my lie about needing to teach American history, but she saw right through it.

"Not loving Mr. Cooper's fine pedagogy, eh? I don't normally take on student teachers, but it sounds like you're in a bind. You can start on Monday."

The first few days, I was overjoyed to be in a place that resembled a real classroom. Ruth knew her stuff and kept the kids under her thumb, even if her teaching methods weren't particularly inspired. But I soon learned that the unspoken price of admission for being her student teacher was lending a sympathetic ear to her life story. Before and after classes (and sometimes during), she talked about her life, a story worthy of a Lifetime movie: a physically abusive grandmother, service in the Israeli army, unfulfilled aspirations as a printmaker, a no-goodnik ex-husband, and troubles raising her uncommonly brilliant son all alone. She did have it hard and they were fascinating stories, but listening to them soon became exhausting.

Ruth was prone to crazy mood swings; she was at times June Cleaver, at times Joan Crawford. And like Mr. Cooper, she, too, could spin some world-class tangents. A lecture on Reconstruction somehow led to probably apocryphal stories of her younger days competing on the bodybuilding circuit. "Have I told you all about the time Arnold Schwarzenegger beat out my friend in competition by spiking his body oil with acid? It's true!" The kids looked befuddled.

Nor did she let the facts of history get in the way of her ego. "Hey miss, you told us no African Americans signed that thingy for equal rights for women, but the book says Sojourner Truth did," said a feisty and bright girl named Tanya one morning as she tugged on a big hoop earring.

Ruth gave a tight, pained smile. "That book is wrong, honey." Case closed.

As I was settling in with Ruth, I got an e-mail from Dr. Renzolli, the young adjunct professor responsible for evaluating student teachers, announcing the date of my first formal classroom observation. Sharp and enthusiastic, she was one of the few professors in the department who had actually taught in a tough city high school in recent years. I cleared it with Ruth, and she gave me the unenviable task of teaching several constitutional amendments; the direct election of senators was the most exciting of them. Yikes.

The day of the observation arrived. With Ruth's guidance, I had overprepared and overthought everything. I stood behind her desk and started the class in a voice so nervous and unfamiliar I wondered whose it was. In the middle of the lesson I looked up from too many pages of notes and scanned the aisles. The kids had the same dead-eyed look as they did in Mr. Cooper's class. A wave of nausea broke over me. It was easy to critique him, but so much harder now that I was up there. Only Tanya answered my questions, and her answers weren't even in the ballpark. By the end of class, Ruth was putting out fires in the back of the room, where boredom was breeding widespread disruption.

Ruth squinted and smiled at me. "Nice work," she whispered. Professor Renzolli thought differently. She took me aside in the hallway afterward and gave me a dose of tough love.

"I know you were trying in there, but you have to realize this isn't a law school seminar. You have to really break it down for these kids."

Too embarrassed to look at her, I scribbled down her comments on top of a *We the People* textbook I was balancing on one knee.

"You used the words *antipathy* and *intractable* without defining them. You aren't talking politics with your friends at a dinner party here."

"Did I really?" I winced. I wanted to think I was above that kind of novice mistake.

"Most of those kids are reading at a sixth-grade level. This," she said, waving a dense handout I had created, "isn't relevant to them."

"I see." I nodded.

"You can't just stand there and talk at them. *Engage* them." She exhaled for a long time and then lightened her tone. "But look, these are bush-league errors. I'm sure you'll do better next time." Again, it wasn't easy for me to accept criticism from someone so much younger (and with tattoos), but she was right.

For the rest of the week I licked my wounds, but I resolved that that first lesson would be my sole misfire. As I stood making photocopies for Ruth on that Friday afternoon, I was surprised to see an unopened digital projector box on a shelf above the copier. I hadn't seen any teacher use so much as a filmstrip at the school, forget about the Internet.

I poked my head into Mr. Frank's office and asked if I could use it. "Oh, that thing? Yeah, all yours. Nobody's found any use for it."

Two weeks later, Professor Renzolli returned for her second observation of me, this time for a lesson on the Gilded Age. As the kids filed into the room, I took the cap off the projector, revealing a gritty Jacob Riis photo of homeless little boys sleeping over a sewer grate, huddled for warmth. All eyes went to the screen and their chatter stopped dead.

"Who's those dirty lil' kids?"

"Poor babies!"

"Why don't they got no shoes?"

I took a deep breath, summoned some theatrical juice from my high school musical days, and launched in.

"In 1848, a journalist called the city of Pittsburgh 'hell with the roof ripped off,'" I said, then hit them with more images of urban squalor in rapid succession.

"Into that hell walked a poor little boy from Scotland named Andrew Carnegie." I flashed a picture of child laborers in factories hunched over menacing machines. "He walked out of that hell as the second-richest man in the world." In quick succession, I clicked through images of his many mansions and castles.

"Ladies and gentlemen of room 717, I ask you, in what kind of country can such extreme things happen?" The next forty-five minutes went by in a flash. The kids oohed and aahed and asked lots of questions. There wasn't a hint of trouble.

Tanya had the last word, and it was on the mark: "So there were a couple of superrich people and a whole lot of superpoor. It's just like today."

"What an excellent observation, Tanya," I said.

As he zipped up his backpack, a kid named Kasheef, a chronic classroom sleeper who worked the late shift at Burger King, piped up: "Hey mister. Bring that projector thing again tomorrow. Okay?"

Professor Renzolli leaped to her feet with a big grin. "That was fantastic! You had them. Every one of them. They even left talking about the lesson. Bravo."

Now, that was more like it. I'd been fed a steady diet of professional affirmation for years, and even a brief interruption was disturbing. I had learned my lesson about lessons: Gravitas doesn't go over big with fifteen-year-olds, but a little razzle-dazzle goes a long way.

After that day, Ruth let me teach more often. She even asked me to show her how to use the projector. Little by little, I got to know and like many of the kids. I was touched one afternoon when Kasheef asked me in the hall, "Can you come back next year as our real teacher?"

In no time, the semester was over.

My hard work and hours of sympathetic listening to Ruth's problems were rewarded in her final evaluation: "Mr. Boland is one of the brightest future pedagogues I have ever had the pleasure of mentoring in my twenty-five years of teaching."

All the while I'd been student teaching, I was also furiously conducting my search for a full-time job for the fall. Based on my student-teaching experience, I avoided the big old-fashioned schools like Eugene Debs ("failure factories," in education reform parlance) in favor of a new high school model that the city was betting on at the time: the "small schools" movement. The philosophy had been largely conceived by a New York visionary named Deborah Meier, embraced by NYC schools chancellor Joel Klein, and backed by millions of dollars from the Gates Foundation. It sought to break apart the enormous, anonymous public high schools that were so typical in New York and replace them with far smaller ones with no more than one hundred students in a grade. The idea was that the kids would feel part of a tight-knit community, could be held more accountable, wouldn't slip through the cracks, and would graduate at a higher rate. Each school centered its curriculum and activities around a particular theme: the arts, American studies, food, law, sports, technology, and so on. Having attended small Catholic schools where every nun and priest knew your first name, last name, and confirmation name, I thought this made perfect sense. At Eugene Debs, I'd found it disheartening to watch the kids being treated so callously and anonymously day in and day out. Why, I wondered, did they even bother showing up at all?

I got offers from many of these schools, but they all had obvious flaws: A small school in Brooklyn devoted to the violin and dance was packed with mostly rowdy girls and a handful of gay boys, none of them showing the slightest interest in the instrument they toted around all day; a media studies academy housed entirely in the basement of a bigger high school was led by a manic principal in stilettos who spoke so fast I thought she must be on coke; and a school in the South Bronx focusing on community service seemed impressive online but turned out to be little more than a cluster of depressing trailers in an old parking lot.

About a week after I sent my résumé to the Union Street School on Manhattan's Lower East Side, I was called for an interview. Union Street was a new combined middle and high school that had to share a building with two other small schools. When I showed up for the interview, the principal, a woman named Mei Vong, greeted me with a warm smile in the main office. She was affable, funny, and vibrant— I liked her at once. As we walked the halls, she showed an obvious devotion to the students, addressing each one by name. She shared her own harrowing story of escaping Vietnam by boat as a child and struggling in American schools. Overwhelmed by the transition to her new setting, she elected to be mute in public throughout most of her time in school. She had excelled in college studying chemistry and then had devoted her life to educating at-risk kids.

She recited the gospel of reform passionately, and I drank it in: "We're rethinking every aspect of the high school experience and striving to do it better. These kids are so far behind. We owe them nothing less." The other teachers I met there spoke as convincingly as she did.

Because the school had an international studies theme, every teacher was required to have lived abroad. The fact that I had taught English in China for a year gave me a leg up. They were welleducated, young, and worldly; many of them were former Peace Corps volunteers, hippie globe-trotters, or foreign-born. To bond the team and infuse a global ethos, during its first year the entire faculty had spent part of the summer learning German together in Minnesota. They knew their craft and were devoted, but also seemed like the kind of people you would want to grab a beer with. There wasn't a Mr. Cooper anywhere in sight.

Next, Mei led me to a history class taught by a young dynamo named Monica who had turned her room into an Italian Renaissance fair. Students in costume talked about da Vinci's inventions, displayed slides of Michelangelo's frescoes, and haltingly read short passages from Machiavelli's *The Prince*. Almost all the kids were engaged and excited. It couldn't have been more different from the deadly boring, teacher-centered "chalk and talk" approach at Eugene Debs.

As if I weren't dazzled enough, the next visit was to a seventh-grade class conducted by Rebecca Luft, a charismatic and hilarious ex-Mormon English teacher. As odd as it may sound, her secret weapon was that she seemed to teach with love. She was a bottomless font of maternal affection, and her students responded in kind with love and obedience. I had rarely seen a class where the students were that eager to please a teacher. But she didn't fly on just love alone; Rebecca had a masterful command of literacy and lesson planning. She could instinctively smell when and where trouble was brewing and quell it before it got out of hand. I didn't want to leave her room.

Immediately after, it was my turn. I taught a sample lesson I'd prepared to a group of ninth graders. The topic: Was Teddy Roosevelt a Progressive? It involved excerpts from Sinclair's *The Jungle*, role-plays, labor union fight songs, and a namesake teddy bear that held the answer to the lesson in an envelope in its tiny paws. The kids loved it, and the teachers who observed me praised the lesson as "spot-on."

The Union Street School was part of a bold experiment; it had the special designation of being an "autonomous school." Inspired by the innovative and entrepreneurial spirit of charter schools, a principal was given much greater autonomy in how to run the school in terms of hiring, curriculum choice, and management. In exchange, however, the school would be held to a higher standard on a variety of performance measures. The Gates Foundation gave special funding to the school and others like it so they could afford these innovations.

I was thrilled to hear the schedule was different from that of most schools. The job would entail teaching just one subject—ninth-grade World History—three times a day in ninety-minute periods. Duties also included a period of advising students, some administrative responsibilities, and a period for preparation. The standard load was five fifty-minute classes and a preparation period and often involved teaching more than one subject. Because there were a number of first-year teachers at Union Street, Mei stressed that there was a great deal of mentoring, support, and training in place.

I had only two reservations: The thought of a ninety-minute class period for fourteen-year-olds seemed ambitious, even crazy—I knew grad students who couldn't sit still for that long—but Mei assured me the time allowed for "deep learning" and cited some research studies that supported the practice. Also, I thought a small school would have smaller class sizes, but the "small" part referred only to the overall enrollment in the school, no more than one hundred students per grade. There were about thirty kids in each class here, which was typical in most New York City public schools. I'd just have to learn to live with it.

Mei called me with an offer the following morning. "You, my friend, will make a great history teacher." I accepted the job with an immediate and enthusiastic yes. It was everything I wanted—*and* only a twenty-minute bike ride from my apartment. I'd hit pay dirt.

As if that weren't enough good news for the week, I was invited to be the student speaker for my graduate school graduation ceremony, sewed up my 4.0 GPA, and received an e-mail with high praise for my master's thesis. Gabe left me a message that he landed a spot teaching American history at a performing arts school in Upper Manhattan. To top it off, Sam got notice of a major chunk of funding for his first feature film.

That weekend in our apartment, after a celebratory pad thai and a bottle of good red wine, Sam and I did our customary happy dance in the living room like two *Peanuts* characters.

It had all fallen into place so perfectly. I was ready to change lives as a teacher, and I'd get my chance in three short months.

Chapter 3

Nemesis

"Lu Huang, do you agree with Raul that he should be allowed to listen to his iPod and make calls during class?" I asked.

"Yeah," he replied sleepily.

"Why?"

"Cuz."

"Can you give me a more specific reason?"

"Just cuz."

An intense-looking kid named Byron made what sounded like a thoughtful statement, but on account of his extreme mumbling and thick Jamaican accent, I couldn't remotely understand what he was saying.

I smiled, pretended to comprehend, and said, "Would anyone else like to add to that?"

The buzz of a defective fluorescent light overhead was the only response.

This wasn't what I had envisioned for my first day of teaching, but the faculty had been given explicit written directions on what to do during our advisory period: "Position your advisees in a circle, have them take turns reading the school's code of conduct, and then reflect on these ideas as a community in thoughtful dialogue, using some of our approved protocols." "Advisories" were glorified homerooms. I was assigned a group of about fifteen freshman boys who were supposed to check in with me at the beginning and end of each day and spend the half hour before lunch working together on schoolwork, community service projects, and character building. Strangely evocative of an old-school Catholic approach, they were single-sex by design.

That muggy morning, I felt an initial swell of enthusiasm as "my boys" pulled their desks screeching across the floor into a lopsided circle. They were a diverse group: staggeringly different in height (four foot ten to six foot three), weight (bantamweight to near-Sumo), age (thirteen to seventeen; some of the older ones at the ninth-grade rodeo for a third time), and even scent (un-treated teen BO to full fumigation with Axe Body Spray). Just about all of them were from working poor families in public hous-ing, but there were exceptions: One boy, Jamal, was living with his mother in a homeless shelter; while another, Lucas, was from "brownstone Brooklyn" and had two professional parents. To my surprise, they came from every borough in the city; some com-muted more than an hour from the Bronx, while others could see their apartments from the school. Skin color ranged from ebony (a boy they called "African Adeyemi") to near-albino ("I'm Puerto Rican but got Irish pirate in me"); severely asthmatic Norman brought up the middle with his own special shade of green-gray. Although mostly black and Latino, the kids were of many eth-nicities, nationalities, races, and racial mixes—with one glaring exception: Caucasian. Similar to Eugene Debs, I identified only one white child in the entire school. As with so many New York City public schools, it was as if *Brown v. Board of Education* or de-segregation had never occurred. (Today, New York's schools are *the* most racially segregated in the Union; even Mississippi and Alabama are more integrated.)

My advisees had fallen into line and were taking turns listlessly reading from a rule book whose cover featured this tagline: "This isn't your old school, things are different here at Union Street." It cataloged all the no-no's: no electronics in sight or in use, no hats, no sunglasses, no gang wear, no inappropriate language, no fighting, blah, blah, blah. The list seemed endless. As we "reflected as a community," I noticed a couple of distracting flashes of red at the door. I turned back to the circle.

And then there was a dull thud, followed by a crash. Near the door he had just kicked open stood one Kameron Shields in pure renegade glory, a one-man violation of every possible rule. Above the neck alone, he was flaunting four violations: He wore sunglasses and a baseball cap over a red bandanna over iPod headphones. A silver flip phone was clipped to his baggy jeans. Everything he wore was cherry red—the hallmark color of the Bloods. I didn't know much about gangs, but even I knew that.

He turned his grinning face to the ceiling and howled, "WASS…UP…NIGGAS?" About half of the boys bleated with laughter at this spectacular entrance; the other half seemed as puzzled as I was. He charged toward the circle and double-high-fived the boys who clearly knew this local hero. I surmised that his fans had all attended middle school with him here at Union Street. I stood in front of him before he could complete his round of glad-handing.

He turned 90 degrees toward one of his buddies, Fat Clovis, looked me up and down, and asked, "Who dat?" His question had a ring of genuine curiosity. I started the morning with first-day jitters made worse with too much caffeine; I was now approaching full-blown panic. My palms got clammy and my mouth sour.

"Hey, somebody forgot to tell this nigga that it's supposed to go like *this*." He took his index finger and made a fucking motion into his rolled-up fist, while simulating what I supposed was a female orgasm.

"Mister," he continued, staring at me, "it don't go like *this*." He clumsily jammed the tips of his two index fingers together and accompanied the motion with falsetto male groans. Christ, I had barely said a word. Could he really smell the gay on me that readily? I'm bent, but I'm not Richard Simmons.

Another wave of laughs. I wanted to assure him that gay sex was a hell of a lot more fun than he was making it out to be, but instead I scrambled to figure out a way to shut him down.

"What's your name?" I barked.

"Nemesis."

"Well, Nemesis," I said, summoning what I thought a real teacher would say, "you can't just walk in here like that and disrupt this class."

Two years of graduate school and six months of student teaching offered me little to draw from. I had taken courses in lesson planning, evaluation, psychology, and research. Next to nothing was said about what a first-year teacher most needs to know: how to control a classroom. What little I had heard was wildly contradictory, a mix of folk wisdom, psycho-jargon, wishful thinking, animal training, and out-and-out bullshit. Most of what I'd learned wasn't even from my professors, but from the shell-shocked first-year teachers I shared my classes with. The majority of our professors hadn't taught in a public school in ages, if ever. One confessed she left teaching not long after being stabbed in the eye with a pencil. Another encouraged me, off the record, to call parents in the hopes of their using serious corporal punishment on the kids at home. "They'll take care of business in a way you can't," he said with a wink.

As I stood staring at young Kameron "Nemesis" Shields's lightly pimpled and peach-fuzzed face, a chorus of voices shouted ten different sets of directions at once inside my head:

Never use sarcasm with kids. You'll just get it back fivefold.

Kids can smell fear, just like dogs can. Stay cool in a crisis.

At the first sign of real trouble, throw a freakin' fit. Make a scene. Kick the garbage can, pound the desk. Make it clear you're the boss, and the boss is pissed off.

Choose your battles carefully. It's a 180-day war. Don't escalate too quickly. You only have so much ammo.

Look, white boy, you gotta channel your inner angry black mama. Develop a churchy, righteous voice of anger. They'll recognize that voice all the way back to the womb.

Those battle-axe nuns in parochial school had it right: "Don't crack a smile until Thanksgiving." You can lighten up as the year goes by, but start out tough and then ease up.

Teachers who make genuine connections with kids don't have to resort to being disciplinarians.

Not one of these nostrums seemed useful at that particular moment. Kameron and I stood face-to-face in showdown pose.

He laughed. "I can't come in here and do that? Well, it looks like I just did, don't it?" He had me there.

Christ! I was leaking credibility fast, a tanker run aground. I had been warned that the way you handle your first big public confrontation with a kid was key. I knew the day would come, but I just wasn't expecting it three hours into my new career.

"Well, it was nice of you to come here to advisory period and show us everything we shouldn't do at Union Street. We needed a real-life example, so I appreciate your help," I said. My humor had worked magic in tense office situations in the past, but here it got me nowhere. There wasn't even a titter from the kids. Just silence.

This kid obviously had far more practice with these kinds of scenes than I did. We locked eyes. His gaze was unflinching, mine wandered nervously. His breathing was slow and steady, mine fast and shallow. This was *his* classroom and, apparently, I had just mistakenly wandered in.

The clock hit 12:30 p.m. and everyone scurried out to lunch in a hurry, laughing all the way.

"That Kameron, man. He is one outrageous nigga," mused Fat Clovis.

I bolted into the faculty lounge and sought out a few of the veterans. "Who is this Kameron Shields?" I asked, and then in an attempt to camouflage my fear in humor: "And why isn't he chained to a rock somewhere?" There was a range of frowns, laughs, and moans.

Everyone burst forth with a witticism or story in quick succession:

"Oh, you met dear Kameron, did you? He was the pride of the middle school here," said Monica with a sheepish smile.

"Oh yeah, he's brutal. He threw an electric pencil sharpener at Miss Dimitriopolou's head last year. That should have gotten him expelled, but our fearless leader thinks it's a failure to throw any kid out," added Marquis, the sophomore history teacher.

"He's still here? I thought he followed his girlfriend to New Jersey. She needed all that dental work. In Jersey, Medicaid has much better dental benefits. Who knew? Maybe I should move there," quipped Rebecca, the middle school reading teacher, as she fiddled in jest with a molar.

I learned more in private from Sita, the guidance counselor-slash-social worker. Kameron was crushed by the departure of his adviser from last year, a young, charismatic science teacher who had made Kameron his pet project. It later turned out that the teacher himself had a problem with authority that manifested itself in pathological lying and rumored weed dealing. And I was not surprised to learn that Kameron's home life was in shambles.

It was only a matter of days before the harsh reality of so many of these kids' lives tumbled out. Kids were being raised by step–half cousins, by foster parents, or in group homes while their parents were in jail, in a shelter, in a mental ward, in Santo Domingo, in labor, in a deportation center in New Jersey, in rehab (again), in Iraq dodging IEDs. All to say, with their lives in pieces. At first, many of their families' choices seemed foolish or reckless, but I quickly realized just how few choices they had.

I thought back to my own school years, but I had no point of comparison. Sure, there were some moments of neglect and embarrassment. In fourth grade, my bargain-hunting mother sent me to school in cheap cardboard shoes from a store worse than Woolworth's. As soon as they touched the slushy playground, they decomposed into shit-brown clumps, leaving me practically stocking-footed and humiliated underneath the monkey bars. But hey, my mother was there soon enough with a hug and a kiss, and a slightly less cheap pair of shoes. And yes, she contributed to my status as a weirdo when, during her brief hippie phase, she refused to buy regular brown paper lunch bags, and forced us instead to use giant paper grocery bags to carry the deeply weird food she packed: something called yogurt that no one at the Sacred Heart School had ever seen before, leftover veal stroganoff in a paper cup secured with a tangle of rubber bands and foil, whole unwashed carrots with the dirt still on them and the green fronds poking out the top of the bag. I longed for Fritos and Ding Dongs, not only for their satisfyingly trashy flavor, but as clear signs of membership in the mainstream. While other children paid the music teacher with a typewritten check in an envelope, I produced a knotted Wonder Bread bag of crumpled singles, quarters, and dimes. "Tell your mother I don't take change," the teacher grumbled. But these were the worst I could conjure. What could I say or do in the face of the horrible deprivation so many of my students faced?

Kameron's reign of terror continued over the next few weeks, and he saved his worst antics for my advisory period. One of the first lessons I'd learned in student teaching was that often the most fearsome streetsy-looking kids were really sweethearts. All the tough trappings were just defenses, just "frontin'," as the kids would say. Often, the students in the polo shirts and nerdy glasses were the ones you had to watch. But not Kameron. He looked like trouble and he was. I was genuinely afraid of him from the minute I set eyes on him. Behind his contraband red-tinted sunglasses, he had a dead-eyed look that unsettled me, and I could tell he liked it that way.

But just when I thought I had him summed up as an unalloyed sociopath, Kameron would show his lighter side. One day before lunch, he was sitting in a corner when he pulled Fat Clovis onto his lap and started fondling him. As I tried to break it up, he cupped Fat Clovis's considerable (and pointy) man-breast in his hand and said, "Mister, look at those tits; they are just perfect. Any bitch in this school would kill to have a rack like this." He kissed one reverently and Fat Clovis giggled. The rest of the boys were howling with laughter. It took all I had not to laugh while I tried to reprimand him.

I stupidly used the word *misogyny* as I scolded him, which earned me the unironic response, "Who is Miss Agany?"

Another day, I actually got him to write a few short sentences. No one in the faculty room could believe it until I produced evidence. "Oh, it's real. He wrote once for me last year, too. See, he writes only in red, like a real Blood should," said Miss Dimitriopolou.

A week later, a visitor appeared in my class. "How's it going?" Mei asked me as she stood in my doorway. All the first-year teachers were struggling mightily and she was making some triage stops after school. She was right to be worried: One right-out-of-college newbie, Alvin the Spanish teacher, abruptly resigned after a month, citing health concerns (though most of us thought he was just pulling the escape cord).

"If you really want to know the truth, I feel like I am standing in front of a tsunami with a mop," I said. She chuckled.

"Really, how's it going?" she pressed. Even though she was the boss, Mei projected such empathy and understanding that I wasn't afraid to unload on her.

"Well, two textbooks were thrown out the window—though you knew that—and someone vandalized my overhead projector with lipstick yesterday. Keeping kids engaged for ninety minutes is difficult. I'm afraid not much 'deep learning' is happening."

"Don't be discouraged. They are testing you. You'll get it under control. I have every faith in you." She tugged on my shoulder until I cracked a smile.

"And then today Kameron Shields threatened to blow up the school."

She shuddered. "Are you serious? Really? He said, 'blow it up'?"

"Twice," I said slowly, "but he was only joking. He's actually done far, far worse than that."

Her hands shot up in alarm. "You don't understand. This is different. After Columbine and 9/11, there are federal laws about this. I am mandated to report this way, way up the chain."

Mei had seen so much bad behavior in her career that I thought she was unflappable. I had never seen her so panicked. What had I unleashed?

"I'm sure he wasn't serious," I said, trying to reassure her. "He threatened to mow down Porter with an Uzi on the first day of school. I don't think he meant that either." I felt my face grow warm. This was going to attract a lot of unwanted attention. Couldn't I just fail privately? And, if I was really honest with myself, I was afraid of a reprisal from Kameron.

"It doesn't matter if he was joking. That kind of threat requires mandatory reporting."

Without knowing it, I had pinged a domino, and suddenly they all came tumbling down. Mei notified the regional superintendent, who in turn notified Homeland Security. Twenty-four hours later, a police sergeant and a patrolman had been summoned to the school. I was pulled out of my class in a hurry.

I entered the principal's office and there sat Mei, the cops, Kameron, and Kameron's sister, who didn't appear that much older than him. But in his sad web of family ties, she was somehow his guardian. She was whimpering; used Kleenexes were piled in a pink pyramid in front of her.

"Mommy's too sick for you to be pullin' this shit, Kameron. You're killing her with all this stupid stuff."

"It was just a joke, man," he kept repeating. He showed the closest thing to fear I had ever seen on his face. Mei recited the turn of events from a folder.

The two cops—the patrolman looked like Channing Tatum, the sergeant like Police Chief Wiggum—then pulled me out into the hall. "So tell me, based on your experience, is that kid in there gonna blow up this school?" asked the sergeant.

"Officer, my experience with kids goes back exactly two weeks." They looked at each other warily. "He is a punk with a real mouth on him, probably a bit of a sociopath, but no, he isn't going to blow up this school."

"That's all we need to hear," said the patrolman. We returned to the office like a jury that had just deliberated.

"Kameron, this teacher here just saved you from getting arrested," said the sergeant. Kameron looked up at me, flashing his dark shark eyes. Maybe, knowing this, he would cut me some slack. *What is going on in there?* I wondered. An emotional volcano, numbed silence, death threat, or gratitude? Who could know?

I went to the grimy windowless teacher's bathroom and pushed my way into the stall. Somebody needed to rein this kid in, to show him that his actions hurt people, but it killed me that of all his offenses, this dumb technicality was the thing that was going to get him in real trouble. It seemed unfair, and, worse, it would allow him to feel wronged by the system, like a victim.

Cops, gangs, threats, Homeland Security? I was in way over my head. And, in a weird way I felt like *I* had done something terribly wrong. I put my head in my hands. I wadded up toilet paper and wiped the tears out of my eyes before they could run down my face. I'd be damned if the kids were going to see me puffy-eyed and weepy over Kameron.

Soon enough, the official word came down from Mei: Kameron would be shipped off to a suspension center in the South Bronx for two months. He would have to commute an hour and a half each way and sit all day in a run-down trailer that served as a classroom in the Harris High School parking lot with other delinquents he didn't know and a couple of burned-out teachers.

I secretly hoped I might earn a little credibility with the kids since I was the first teacher in the three-year history of Union Street who managed to get Kameron suspended, though many had tried. But no such luck: I had sold their hero up the river on a trumped-up charge. Despite my victory, the damage he had done to my reputation that first day was beyond repair. Instead of the gay witch hunt dying down after he was gone, as I'd hoped, the rest of the boys declared open season on me in his name. To confirm what both Chantay and Kameron had insinuated, they took the trouble to conduct a battery of oblique questions about my girlfriends (none); appetite for contact sports (zero); and other butch hobbies (only opera and gourmet cooking). They never asked me point-blank if I was gay or not, but they came to the correct conclusion. In case I had any doubt as to what was going on, someone scrawled on a bulletin board outside my room, "Payback is a bitch. Boland is a bitch."

I contemplated making a public coming-out statement, but I didn't want to generate more attention and enmity with a dramatic announcement in my first few months. There were already enough distractions. Advice from my coworkers—both straight and gay—was again wildly contradictory, ranging from "Are you crazy?" to "Why put blood in the water?" to "Own it publicly and the issue will disappear!" to "I dunno." Sam, who was nearly tossed out of Yale for his militant AIDS activism, encouraged me to bite the bullet and come out. Unsure of what to do and lacking my usual confidence, I decided to say nothing.

Stories of Kameron in exodus filtered back to Union Street. In the Bronx, without backup in non-Blood territory, he was repeatedly jumped. He started to carry weapons. When it was almost time for him to come back, a group of us made an unsuccessful appeal to the union to try to block his return. The only advice they could offer the ninth-grade teachers was the ludicrous idea of contacting our local police precinct and registering a complaint against him. This was the best the union could offer? We'd be laughed out of the precinct.

When he came back months later, he was even angrier, but he managed to curb his worst behavior for a short time because he knew he had used up his chances.

Two weeks after his return, as Kameron was bounding up the stairs to class one morning, a hammer fell out of his pocket and directly into the path of Trey, the bearded sophomore English teacher. A hammer was contraband in its own right, but this one also concealed a double switchblade. It was the last straw. Kameron was gone for good.

At dismissal that day, I overheard Fat Clovis's pithy take on the situation: "Oh. They getting real tough around here now. Three hundred strikes, you out." He was trying to be outlandish, but his count probably wasn't far off.

CHAPTER 4

Nowhere Over the Rainbow

KAMERON WASN'T THE only surprise I encountered on day one. During the final period of my first day, I was working my way through the attendance list. To avoid the sins of my student-teaching "mentor," Mr. Cooper, who mangled every ethnic name he ever came across, I went to great pains to pronounce everyone's name correctly, consulting veteran teachers and even scribbling phonetic approximations in the margins of the roster. Given that the kids hailed from everywhere from Yemen to Haiti to Malaysia, it was no easy feat. Nigerian names are particularly notorious among teachers. Kamiolakamioluwalamibe, anyone? (In case you are wondering, as I did, it means "We appeal to God for help" in Yoruba. Indeed.)

I was close to the end of the list with no obvious gaffes, so I was surprised to hear so much laughter after a name as simple as "Leon Washington."

In response, a timid, prim "Here" was delivered into the ether.

More snickering. I looked up.

My eyes followed a set of long, tapered fingers past a bent wrist, down a thin caramel arm to the face of a pretty, doe-eyed boy. Unlike any other kid in class, he wore a natty polo shirt with a popped collar. Not a hint of wannabe gangster on him. I tried to suspend my snap judgments, but two things flashed in my head: First, Gay with a capital G. And then, jeez, what a burden for a kid like that to have to walk around with such a macho NFL-esque name like Leon Washington.

I clearly wasn't the only one who thought this way.

"Is that your name for real, baby? You sure don't look like no Leon Washington," sneered Chantay. That got a laugh.

"Dead ass, Dead ass," said someone in a new-to-me slang term of affirmation.

"Hey, pipe down," I reprimanded, borrowing an old naval expression I'd heard from my father growing up.

Another wave of laughter. Little did I know that "pipe down" was now a street expression for sex, akin to "laying pipe." Oops. So many new words to learn.

I cruised through two more names without incident and then came to the last one:

"Mariah Wilks?"

"Mariah!" someone said in a mocking, pop-vocal way, trying to jump an octave or two.

Of course, I couldn't help but think of the pop star. With such an aspirational name, I was on the lookout for a glam girl and scanned the aisles for some mother's ultimate fan tribute. But, as far as I could tell, just about everyone was accounted for, except for a boy in a red hoodie at the back of the room with his head on the desk, who had slipped in at the very last minute. Slowly, he picked up his head.

I took a quick look and followed my instincts honed from summers spent with butch lesbians on the beaches and in the bars of Fire Island.

"Are you Mariah?" I asked. Even at fifteen paces, it was clear to me that Mariah was a girl who wasn't very much interested in looking like a girl. To confirm my hunch, I scanned for an Adam's apple but didn't see one. As familiar as I was with gender bending in all its glorious forms, I was still pretty surprised to see it on such bold display here in ninth grade at Union Street. This wasn't a queer-friendly college campus like Oberlin or Reed where binary gender choices were regarded as passé.

"Yup," she responded in a low growl.

More from Chantay. "Wow. Mister, you the first new teacher ever to figure out she's a girl!" Unlike Leon, no one laughed at Mariah. Many of the kids had been with her at Union Street for middle school, and I guessed that they all knew better than to mock her.

Mariah looked pouty and mean, like a cranky baby who had just woken up from a nap. She was square-shaped, dark-skinned, and had poorly kept cornrows, which revealed a scalp shiny from perspiration. Despite the stifling heat in the room, she wore several layers under her hoodie. With a cocky swagger, she arched over the back-rest of her desk and spread her legs farther apart than any boy.

In the early days of the semester, I watched Leon and Mariah both closely, on the lookout in case either of them was bullied. I wanted to make sure it didn't happen on my watch. Of course, I didn't really know the true sexual orientations of these children and it wasn't my business, but I couldn't pretend it wasn't a factor either. Given the affinity, I thought I might identify with them more, or at least want to advocate for them if they needed it.

At first I saw little to concern me. Despite my initial gay hazing by Kameron, I got the sense this generation was more tolerant. They had grown up on a steady diet of gay-friendly media with Ellen, Rosie, *Will & Grace*, and *The L Word*. And even if they were young, gay issues had been swirling everywhere around them in the zeitgeist: Don't Ask, Don't Tell; same-sex marriage; and the bittersweet visibility that came with the AIDS epidemic. I thought back to Javan, the militantly queer kid in Mr. Cooper's class at Eugene

Debs. If anything, he was the bully who terrorized the straight boys .
with withering comments, not the other way around.

Aside from the occasional ribbing, Mariah appeared tolerated by
all, admired by many, and feared by most. Leon also seemed to be
fine. He hung around with a small but tight super-girlie-girl posse;
they walked the halls together, ate at the same lunch table in the
cafeteria, and all seemed to giggle in unison. I had to stifle a laugh
one day when I overheard him describing a sweater as "not really
magenta, I'd have to say...more fuchsia" to his buddy Talia. Even
more surprising, he inflected it with suburban-girl upspeak and a
touch of raspy "vocal fry." Where had this kid from the South Bronx
picked that up?

Both Leon and Mariah were playing to type in the extreme,
which ran smack up against my post-gay-liberation hopes for the
world. I harbored ludicrous stereotype-reversing fantasies that
would cause the entire class to rethink their assumptions: Maybe
Leon would turn out to be a sensational running back or Mariah
would suddenly rock a pretty floral skirt in class. I wanted to throw
out my lesson on Indian geography and give a high school–
appropriate rendition of "Free to Be...You and Me." One where I
would sing about my gay friends who had played in the NFL, rose
through the ranks of the Marines, or laid bricks for a living. About
the lesbians I had known who had never so much as touched a soft-
ball bat or looked under the hood of a car.

After about a month, however, it became clear that my early in-
terpretation of the social scene as generally tolerant was wrong. In
retrospect, I can see that the first few weeks of ninth grade are just
a period of unspoken détente, a time for human data collection. Underneath the quiet surface, the social hierarchy was being formed:
Cliques were crystallizing, pecking orders established, and judgments made. Kids pegged one another as smart or naughty, ugly

or "fly," outrageous or "BORIN!" Their determinations were based on a complex algorithm that factored in your ethnicity, weight, borough, sneaker choice, level of bling, your churchiness, your potty mouth, the depth of your cleavage, and the arc of your ass. And your social history from middle school, if known, was another factor. (Despite being the putative class beauty, Milagros would never, ever rise to be queen bee because she had inexplicably wet her pants in seventh grade.)

The results of this grand formula seemed final and strangely unanimous. What strange creatures we are that we do this almost instinctively. I suppose it helps us feel more secure about our place in the world.

In the final analysis, though, Mariah emerged near the top of the heap. The girls were indifferent to Mariah and the guys liked her. She could hang. With them she shared an obsession with sports, a gravitational pull toward thug life, and an unspoken but palpable interest in the ladies.

As much as she was a star in the social firmament, Mariah was a nightmare in the classroom, treating me and the other teachers with contempt from the beginning. She was wildly disruptive and didn't do a lick of work. She had two settings: rage and mischief, with little in between. One afternoon I tried to keep her after class for nailing some boy's head dead-on with an eraser from halfway across the room. I got in her face about it and she bellowed back at me. She flipped over a desk and an easel and ran out the door.

What made it all worse was that Mariah was what I would call "crypto-smart": She would show you on the sly that she was capable of absorbing any idea, doing any assignment, but then she made it clear that, out of spite, she would do nothing academic. One October afternoon, after no one offered to answer a tough question I posed about the Silk Road, I turned to write on the board. Out of nowhere Mariah interjected, "It was an exchange of goods, but also of ideas."

I spun around, stunned.

"You liked that, didn't you?" she said, toying with me. And then it was back to havoc-making. In the course of seven seconds, I went from a surge of hope to flat-out disenchantment. Welcome to teaching in ninth grade.

Meanwhile, the campaign against Leon, who had ended up near the bottom of the social order, was escalating. At first it was just the occasional snarky comment about his voice, walk, or clothes. That was followed by ugly notes addressed to "the cocksucker" and graffiti ("Leon = fag face"). Then I heard he was getting shoved in the hallway, openly mocked in gym.

At the same time, I was getting the adult version of the same treatment. Not for a second did I expect my students to welcome a gay teacher with open arms, especially not a white rookie. After all, many of the "good" kids were the children of fire-breathing evangelicals, and many of the "bad" ones had been born during the height of the AIDS epidemic to homophobic parents. But I was armed with two decades of activism, therapy, and identity politics. In my day, I had been called everything from a sodomite to a turd burglar. What could some high school freshmen say that I hadn't heard before? Sticks and stones...

It turns out, they could say, "Mr. Boland is a faggot." They could say it a dozen times in a week, in lots of ways, in different languages and dialects. They could say it stone-cold to my face or frothing as they were being hauled out of my classroom screaming. The first, the fifth, the fifteenth lash didn't really penetrate. But over the next few months, the hate slowly seeped into my bedrock and did some damage. To my surprise, it stuck and it hurt.

I knew it was getting to me one Friday afternoon in November, after a particularly tough week, when I was riding my bike home from school. I had gone out for a few beers with my coworkers in an East Village hipster bar with a cheap happy hour. I was pedaling along, feeling a little drunk but mostly numb. I knew the anger was somewhere in me, but I couldn't place it, couldn't vent it, couldn't puke it out like bad fish. I pulled up behind a city bus going up First Avenue. I was so close to it, I could see the engine rattling behind a metal grille. It threw heat, spit exhaust, and roared suddenly as the bus accelerated. I pedaled frantically behind and started screaming at the engine like a maniac for two whole blocks. I shrieked louder than the roar of the bus, and people on the sidewalk turned wide-eyed to see what was the matter. I pulled off onto a dark side street in between two cars. I closed my eyes, gritted my teeth, and willed my frantic breaths back to normal.

If it was bad for me, it was worse for Leon. A week after my bus breakdown, things came to a head and he was beat down in the lunchroom by three boys. They skipped the usual formality of creating some pretext for the violence (typically something like "That faggot was checking out my ass"), and they just beat him. Word had it that he didn't fight back at all, which only further stained his reputation. Jesús, the ringleader, was hauled off to Mei's office by the school security guards. Mei offered to let Leon go home, but he stayed in school for the rest of the day. He arrived at my class not long afterward. His eyes were puffy from crying, and he looked so scared. My heart went out to the kid. His girlfriends comforted him, while I overheard the boys snarling, "What a little bitch, he didn't even fight back" or "Man up, Leon." As I reprimanded them, Leon sank farther into his seat in embarrassment.

Leon's mother was called to the school the next day. I remembered from parent-teacher conferences that she was a put-together woman with a ready smile. Because he wasn't my advisee, I wasn't at the meeting, but I heard through the grapevine that through her tears she said, "Not again. This happened all throughout middle school. I thought this school would be different. Can't you do something?"

Without mentioning Leon by name, Mei made an announcement to the entire grade the following day about universal respect and nonviolence. She cited the Golden Rule and finished by saying, "It is as important to me that we create a tolerant school community as an academic one." It was heartfelt and moving to adults. The kids, having heard many such talks over the years, shifted in their seats, bored and bothered. They were mentally tuned to a different channel altogether.

What made Leon's situation feel so hopeless was that much of it took place outside of school and our classrooms. The harassment happened during his commute, in his neighborhood, and on the Internet. Worse, I don't think he reported half of what was really happening to him. And in what became a depressing pattern during the year, increased adult attention and concern only seemed to make the bullies more furtive and determined, so it was no wonder he seemed to trust his teachers as little as his tormentors. But among all of the teachers, he was most eager to distance himself from me. I was kryptonite to him, radiating gay guilt by association. He wouldn't make eye contact and barely spoke to me. And so I kept my distance.

I found some small comfort when the English teacher, Porter, told me that in the daily journal he required his students to keep, Leon was opening up. He wrote about how happy it made him to indulge his sweet tooth, his indignation that his mother had to stand in a puddle of piss in the elevator of their project with her grocery cart, and his dream of an adult life where he was a rich and respected pediatrician. I was shocked that some of the most unlikely kids would fill notebook after notebook about what they weren't willing to say out loud, committing their innermost thoughts to paper and risking discovery. The period was as much therapy as English class. I was just glad Leon was communicating somehow.

In early November, the social worker Sita put Mariah's name at the top of the agenda for the ninth-grade-team "kid talk," a structured protocol every three weeks where teachers, advisers, administrators, and the social worker would discuss one child's progress— or the lack thereof—in great depth and brainstorm strategies for how to address problems. It was exactly the kind of thoughtful and innovative practice that a small reform-minded school could do and exactly why I was attracted to Union Street. This would never have happened at a big anonymous place like Eugene Debs. There, teachers would fill out some kind of disciplinary report and it would go into a Bermuda triangle of paperwork, rarely to be answered. There, the kids were lucky if the teachers knew much more than their names.

Around the circle we went with our observations:

"She's missed days and days of school. But when she's here she's failing and fighting," said Bridget, the ninth-grade science teacher.

"The girls in her advisory group tell me she's being recruited for a gang. Makes sense. I'd want her in my gang," the math teacher, Dorothy, said wryly.

Gretchen, our vice principal, said, "There are serious signs of neglect here. It's obvious she doesn't know anything about feminine hygiene. Have you gotten close to her? She positively reeks. And she's wrapped up in that same stinky red hoodie every day. We need to do a serious intervention and get the mother in here right away."

Sita nodded, adding, "I certainly don't want to jump to any conclusions, but it's a potential sign of abuse when kids swaddle themselves up in layers like that, especially when the weather is still warm. It's like they are putting on armor. I've seen it before."

"She's in my first-period class and she smells like pot a lot," said Porter, the English teacher.

"Well, her nickname *is* Wavy," I told him, proud of having learned the day before that it meant a stoner.

We had invited Tasneen, Mariah's eighth-grade reading teacher, to the meeting to give us some background. Tasneen was a former lawyer and midlevel diplomat at the UN who had also turned to teaching in midlife. She said, in her beautiful Persian accent, "I'm afraid to say we had the exact same discussion last year and took a lot of the steps you're discussing. It was to little effect. We don't know much about her home life because I don't think there is much of one. We certainly got no help from the mother last year."

She seemed embarrassed to be breaking the news to us after all our brainstorming. She finished with, "She's the angriest kid in the school."

"Wow. So many are so angry. That's saying a lot," exhaled Sita.

"We need to send a clear signal to the mother. I'll send a certified letter today saying she has to contact the school within three days or else we will involve Child Protective Services," Gretchen said decisively.

Her idea worked. By the next week, the usual gauntlet of teachers and staff had been assembled for a parental intervention meeting. Since her mother had ignored the barrage of calls we made to her, we were ready to read her the riot act.

We sat in the back of the dim and dingy school auditorium in a circle, where we first met alone with Mariah's mother. Gaunt and exhausted-looking, Mrs. Wilks appeared a lot older than the other mothers I'd met, and she didn't look much like her daughter. To our surprise, she was wearing a NYC School Safety Officer uniform. She must have known what it was like to deal with a building full of kids like Mariah. Knowing that she was pretty much in the same business as we were made her neglect seem even worse.

Without waiting for us to begin, Mrs. Wilks started in, speaking in a soft voice: "I'm sorry things are bad with her. I know I'm not home enough, but it's hard alone. I got two more at home, and, God's truth, they aren't much easier than Mariah." She sighed. "I'm at Richmond Heights High on Staten Island. It's an hour and a half each way from Upper Manhattan. And I work another job week-ends, as a home health aide."

Shit from the old and shit from the young, I thought.

Without warning, her voice became pinched, her tone indignant. "You all need to know something. If Protective Services takes my kids, it would kill me. And you know they would be worse off in foster care. I see it all the time in my school."

"Mrs. Wilks, no one here is talking about taking anyone's kids away," Sita reassured her. "Everyone is just concerned about your daughter. She's in serious trouble in a lot of different ways."

"That girl, she just won't listen. I try talking to her. Has a mind of her own. Always has. But I do my best," Mariah's mother protested. I could hear just a hint of the Deep South in her voice.

In the course of three minutes, I went from feeling barely con-tained rage at this woman to utter sympathy for her. There were days before my teaching career when Sam and I would come home exhausted just from taking care of our relatively affluent, educated, and healthy selves. Even after the cleaning lady came and the take-out was ordered, we felt overwhelmed. And we didn't have so much as a goldfish or an air fern to take care of. Who was I to judge this woman?

Sita pushed open the auditorium door and gave a nod to Mariah, who shuffled in and plunked down in the only empty chair. She sat in her usual pose of defiance: arms folded like a bouncer, head cocked to the side, eyes glazed over. After Gretchen cited a long list of offenses, she didn't say a word in her own defense.

"What's wrong, Mariah, why you actin' like this? You know better than all this nonsense, baby," Mrs. Wilks said, her tone maternal and comforting. She touched her daughter's face. It was strange to see Mariah being treated so tenderly, so vulnerably. In the never-ending struggle with her, you could easily forget she was somebody's baby.

Mariah's expression didn't change a bit. But after a long while, slow, thick tears started crawling down her face. No one knew what to say. We waited for a long time; the cheery noise of dismissal rose outside.

She shook her head and whispered, "I dunno, Ma, I dunno."

We ended the meeting with a list of promises and hopes—periodic check-ins, behavior contracts, and referrals to social services. Mariah's mother blankly nodded at all of the ideas, but mostly she just seemed overwhelmed. I shook Mrs. Wilks's hand and watched as she walked away with her daughter. I couldn't shake the feeling that we would never see her mother again and that Mariah would continue to drift into harm's way.

The following week, we were on a field trip to a giant high school science expo in the Javits Convention Center on the west side of Manhattan. Thousands of kids from all over the city roamed the cavernous crystal palace, walking from table to table observing experiments and cutting-edge technology. Our kids were enthusiastic and rowdy. They guzzled experimental energy drinks by the quart and screamed at the Battle of the Robots like they were at a professional wrestling match.

On the perimeter of the madness, I spotted Leon alone on a

bench. He wore a button-down oxford shirt and sat with the perfect posture of a dancer. We were outside of school and none of his classmates were in sight; I thought this might be my opportunity to connect.

"How's it going, Leon?" I asked, sitting on the next bench on purpose to give him some space. I didn't even look at him directly.

"I'm not doing anything wrong," he said indignantly, scanning the area for his classmates.

"I didn't say you were. I just asked how you are."

Nothing.

I let a full minute pass.

"Leon, you don't have to talk to me about anything, but I do want you to know something. I know you are a really good kid and..."

"You don't know me."

I pressed on. "I know you are a good kid and those guys are giving you a really hard time. I'm sorry that is happening. We are trying to stop it."

He folded his arms and sank into a deep pout.

Not a word.

"I just want you to know I am here to talk if you ever want to."

"Leave me alone," he seethed. He got up and started to walk away. I couldn't help but want to throw him another lifeline. I continued, a little bit louder, "Don't be afraid to stand up to them. But I don't mean use violence. And..."

He turned back quickly to me. "Leave me alone. I am not afraid to stand up to anyone." He sounded convincing with me, but I doubted he could summon the same bravado in front of a bunch of ninth-grade bullies.

As he disappeared into the crowd, I was saddened at my failure to help him. But in retrospect, I was probably even angrier at my self-

ish need to be an avenging gay hero. How cliché. Why did it matter
so much to me to help the gay kid anyway? Lots of straight people had stood up for little gay me when I needed it. And there were
other kids who would have welcomed a gesture like this. Why not
put my energy there?

I thought back to one afternoon during the dead of winter in my
junior year in high school. I'd left English class and pushed my way
through a swinging door into the bathroom, where I saw a group of
guys beating up Max Mumford. Then, as now, there was "probably/
passable gay" and "no-hiding-it gay." I was in the former, and he was
clearly in the latter category. Max and I had been on the swim team
together the year before. A sweet kid with a campy sense of humor,
he declared his love of the decorative and festive aspects of Christmas too loudly and paid the price. He looked, sounded, and even
dressed sort of like his skinny suburban mother. If I didn't know better, you'd think they went to the same hairdresser for frosted tips.

Max kept trying to leave the bathroom, pretending his tormentors weren't there. Trying to hold on to his dignity, he didn't say
a word; he wouldn't even look at them. They just kept shoving
him back into a corner, slamming him against the cracked white-
tile wall. I would like to say I boldly intervened to help my gay
brother and then alerted the proper authorities. But instead, I did
what someone who was just one rung higher than Max in the pecking order would do. I took a pee, washed my hands, and walked
out of the bathroom, thinking, *Poor Max.* When I got back to AP
English, my classmates were parsing a scene from *Macbeth* where
the old king rages about cowards and deserters to a young soldier:
"Thou lily-livered boy... Those linen cheeks of thine are counselors
to fear." I was being described to a T.

I winced at the memory as I looked out at the traffic whizzing by on Eleventh Avenue. As an adult, I was obviously more secure and willing to take action, but the end result was the same: Gay kids were still being bullied, and I was no more effective in saving Leon than I'd been in helping Max.

A few days later, we were in class preparing for a debate on the Hindu caste system. Even though I told them I thought it was silly, the kids insisted on forming boy and girl teams. And so, for once, Leon was separated from his usual giggly girl group.

I was making my normal rounds among the groups, navigating the scattered clusters of desks. Leon sat there quietly, ill at ease among a group of first-rate bad boys—an untouchable among the Brahmins. Leon was by no stretch a scholar; he hovered between failure and low 70s all year long. But, by this point, I was at least used to his minimal output—a halfhearted sentence here or a completed multiple-choice question there. Today, his work sheet was totally blank. I knew he was going with the flow, but it ticked me off to see him stoop to their level.

"Leon. Get to work," I ordered him.

"Shut up," he replied, matter-of-factly and not very loud.

"What did you just say?" I said, stunned.

I could hear how shallow and quick his breathing was. Defiance was not his strong suit.

"Shut up," he said again.

Shit. I was being told off in front of the class not just by a "good" kid, but by a gay sister no less. Why didn't I just keep my mouth shut and let him do nothing with the bad boys? I supposed this was some kind of new low, but at that point I didn't have enough energy to rank the humiliations.

The group of boys around him were suddenly wide-eyed. "Leon!"

Somebody gave him a manly, affirming backslap. I don't imagine he'd had many of those in his life. His thin frame had a hard time absorbing it. Leon looked left and right for guidance from the boy posse and sensed they were pleased. He gave them a weak, uncertain smile.

Jesús was elated. "You hear that, everybody?" He stood and announced to the whole class in a voice high with joy, "Leon just grew a set of balls! He told Mister to step the fuck down."

How did my gay-empowerment speech to Leon get turned against me? Why would he defy one of his few allies? I guess he stood up to one of the few people he thought he could. Maybe this was some kind of twisted progress on his way to self-empowerment. But mostly I was just livid. *I* wanted to call him a little bitch, and worse.

I pulled out a futile response from my menu of reprimands: "Jesús, be quiet. You listen to me, Leon. You get yourself right and get some work done." He bowed his head down.

Even though I should have, I couldn't bring myself to call Leon's mother or write up a disciplinary report. I told myself I didn't want to trouble or confuse her, but, at heart, I didn't want to admit to her or anyone else that it had even happened.

The next day was Saturday, and Sam had just finished shooting his feature film that week. There was much to celebrate and lots of friends to thank for everything from serving as extras to providing legal advice to baking brownies, so we spontaneously threw a big brunch.

In quick succession, the buzzer rang and in rolled the bohemian gay-bourgeoisie and their affiliates: Josh, the brilliant, frenetic law professor; Ben, the devoted AIDS activist and media guru; his new boyfriend, Wilfredo, a perfectionist events maven; and Johan, a mad biochemist with a hangover. On hand for the lesbians were our closest couple friends, Karen and Kat; and Tracy represented the straight world. Over mimosas, we heard war stories from Sam about the last two weeks of film production. We laughed about his bribing a drunken building super to get access to an apartment and firing a clueless production assistant who was overheard calling one of the actresses a "twat."

About an hour into the raucousness, our friend Daniel, whom I hadn't seen since the school year began, arrived right off a red-eye from San Francisco. With his long, flaming red hair, pink raincoat, and his one-eyed Shih Tzu in tow, his entrance was hard to ignore. Both he and the dog were in rare form, highly medicated on pills after the flight.

He made his way to the table and looked at the modest offerings: scrambled eggs, toast, and coffee.

"Are we at a truck stop?"

"There's cheese in the eggs," I said defensively.

He arched his eyebrow in concern and turned to the assembled guests. "The last time I was here for brunch you made duck jambalaya and lamb liver pâté. This is a cry for help!" He waved his hand over the kitchen table.

"Are you okay, kitten?" he asked. I was quiet.

He turned to Sam. "Is he okay?" Sam looked down, saying nothing.

"Teaching's been pretty exhausting," I said.

He turned to Sam again. "I gotta say, he looks like shit."

"I'm not sleeping very well," I said.

He put out his arms, "Come, tell Mama all about it." The rest of the clan gathered around me on the couch. They had all been thinking these things for the last three months, but Daniel actually said them.

I gave a grim recap of the year so far and, knowing that my

audience would be particularly interested in Leon and Mariah, recounted their tales in detail. Our friends were saddened and riveted at the same time.

"Why would you stay in that goddamn place another minute? I went to schools like that in Chicago. Get out. No need to be a martyr," said Wilfredo.

"So let me get this right," Daniel said. "You have the baby lesbian terrorizing you one minute and breaking down in tears the next. And a gay-boy-in-training telling you off after you try to help him. That is messed up!"

"So much for gay solidarity," said Josh.

Tracy sighed. "It's so sad. Kids see anybody who's different and immediately they start to bully."

Karen, who ran a youth service organization, jumped in: "No, I don't think that's it. It's really about power, not about being different. The girl sounds every bit as different as the gay boy does, but they don't bully her because they see her as powerful. The boys think being gay means you've given up the privilege of being a 'real' man. They're punishing him for leaving the boys' club and rewarding her for leaving behind the 'weaker' gender. It's just another form of misogyny."

It made perfect sense. These kids had so little power, they couldn't believe anyone would give it up willingly. "You're right," I told her. "In the school where I did my student teaching, there was a boy who was every bit as femmy as Leon, but he was a thug. And nobody fucked with him."

There was a long silence. It was all true and insightful, fascinating even. I used to love these kinds of conversations—in a college seminar or over a glass of wine with friends talking about a *New Yorker* article. But in less than forty-eight hours, I would be back at school and dealing with the ugly reality of it all. I felt dizzy.

The crowd started to thin out. As they exited, each had a loving word of encouragement or a turnaround anecdote that they shared with me. Daniel was the last to leave, and he held me in a long embrace by the door.

"Hey, babe, I don't know jack about teaching, but I do know this: You will figure this out. And you are having a way more positive effect on these little shits than you know. Hang tough. I love you."

He cinched his colorful Guatemalan peasant pants, picked up his one-eyed dog, and sauntered out.

I started to collect plates and pour half-finished mimosas down the kitchen drain. I thought about the week ahead, certain it would be another of chaos and cruelty. But Daniel's words and the collective display of love from my friends stirred me. As I loaded the dishwasher, I reassured myself with affirming bursts in quick succession: It was still early in the year. I had fought uglier monsters in my life. They were just kids, just people with fears and needs like all of us. It was important work. It wouldn't be easy, but I would rally and figure it out.

CHAPTER 5

Powers of Ten

"LISTEN UP, EVERYBODY. I've got big news. On our next test, everyone is getting a 100."

It was only October, but getting my students' attention had become nearly impossible. That week alone I had resorted to shouting, flashing the lights, and, at the suggestion of Gretchen, our Buddhist-convert vice principal, clanging together brass temple cymbals. Nothing worked. This announcement, however, stopped their chatter cold.

"Wha— What?" stammered Fat Clovis.

"That's because you are all going to take the test until you get a 100. You might get it all right on the first try, you may take it twenty times, but you are going to keep at it until you get a 100." This unconventional idea was met with lots of suspicion, but among the chronic F crowd, who was going to argue with a guaranteed A? Despite their public statements to the contrary, every one of my kids hated failing.

"Your assignment is to name and spell all the world's continents and oceans." A collective moan filled the room.

"That shit's for babies," said a voice from nowhere.

"For freakin' retards," added another.

"Monkey retards," a third.

"Quiet!" I had grown so tired of chasing down these nonstop, quicksilver asides, I could barely muster a response. "Basic geography is something any educated person is expected to know."

I was following some much-needed advice from my unofficial mentor and heroic colleague Monica, whose tenth-grade history class I had observed a few days before. As her students diligently scribbled away at an assignment, we huddled over her old-school overhead projector and whispered.

"These kids are so used to failing. Make it so they *have to* succeed at something, no matter how basic. Once they taste a little success, you'll win them over, I promise." The bluish glow of the projector illuminated her face and gave her an even more saintly aura of authority.

Whenever I needed a dose of inspiration or advice, I turned to Monica. After all, watching her teach a masterful class on the Italian Renaissance the spring before had convinced me to take the job at Union Street. Despite being twenty-seven years old, five foot three, and even whiter than me in both spirit and complexion, she commanded attention and respect from her students. She knew how to teach kids to read, formed a school singing group, and ran the Model UN. It seemed like she was at school daily from 7:00 a.m. to 7:00 p.m. After graduating from Yale four years before, she could easily have worked for an investment bank or gone to law school; instead, she had been tearing it up in tough public schools.

Given my miserable results so far in our geography unit, I wasted no time trying her "100 for everybody" idea. But it wasn't as easy as it sounded. What I thought would take a day or two at most turned into nearly a week of floundering. Over and over, my students misplaced and misspelled major swatches of the planet on their tests: "Afrika" (if only Dannisha were German); "you-rope" (not a bad start for Yerfrey, a kid fresh off the boat from the Dominican Republic

who spoke virtually no English); and "Ass-ia" (from Merwin, probably confusing it with one of the "me so horny" Asian porn sites he
endorsed so enthusiastically). On the first day of class on his getting-
to-know-you form, he'd written under hobbies in his own unique
spelling, "watching porm." Byron, the class prodigy with a case of
the mumbles, was blasé about receiving a perfect score on his first
attempt. "Well, Mr. Boland, we did this very same assignment when
I was in Jamaica," he quipped, then, after pausing for effect, "in the
third grade." I cringed. How tedious all this must have been for him.

While it was true that this experiment had instilled some confidence in them, the kids were also bored out of their minds. So next
I tried to get creative, thinking back to what intrigued me about
geography as a student. I hit on an idea. When I was in middle
school, our single, intellectually oriented, and probably gay uncle
Bernie took my sisters and me to see Charles and Ray Eames's short
movie *Powers of Ten*. Made in the late 1960s, it's a dazzling display
of the structure of the universe at its most macro and micro. In
magnitudes of ten, the camera zooms out from the image of a couple napping after a picnic on a blanket in Chicago to high above
the city, the planet, and then to the outermost reaches of the universe. Then the action reverses back to the cozy couple and zooms
in on the man's hand, going ever deeper until we are at the cellular,
the molecular, and then even the subatomic level. It's an acclaimed
work that asks deep questions about our place in the world. Besides,
what kid doesn't love seeing a movie in class?

With Sam's help, I worked almost the whole weekend to find the
movie online, illegally download it, buy software that could run it,
secure a projector, and draft a work sheet of related questions. But
I didn't mind. I was sure it was going to be worth the effort, and I
needed a hit.

That Monday I announced, "Forget longitude, forget latitude—

this movie is going to ask you to find your place in the world in a totally different way." My students chatted casually, ignoring me, like passengers indifferent to a flight attendant's safety instructions. My words echoed off the drab orange walls. I clicked Play on my laptop.

Pacing restlessly at the back of the room as the film played, I was shocked at the silence. Were they bored or intrigued? Listless or lost in thought? Only two students seemed obviously interested. Predictably, one of them was good girl Nee-cole, who was always curious about everything, but I was shocked to see that normally dead-eyed Yvette was looking alert for the first time all year, secretly watching from behind her pink backpack. The kids stirred and stretched as I turned on the lights and asked for reactions.

I ignored the first guerrilla outbursts: "corny," "mad old," "terrible special effects." I wasn't too surprised. To this generation, even *Jurassic Park* seemed hopelessly outdated, but I pressed on.

Victor Rosario, a chubby boy with a shaved head and light eyes who had shown no signs of interest in class whatsoever, raised his hand.

"At first I wondered, Why they showin' his hand so close up?" he said deliberately.

"Good observation, Victor. What did you conclude?" I asked.

He smiled widely. "Well, then I thought about it. They showin' it cause...dude can't stop beating off, can't stop pulling it," he replied, jerking his hand wildly and rolling his eyes.

Boys laughed. Girls scowled and cried, "Gross!"

"Enough, Victor. Who has a real question about the film?" I asked.

Silence.

I took a risk. "Yvette, anything you would like to say?"

"Mister, leave me *alone!*" she growled, every word louder than the last. So much for being intrigued. Her classmates catcalled her and she sneered back.

Yvette had been a mystery to me from day one. Tall and lithe, she wore the same pair of supertight blue jeans adorned with butterfly appliqués every day. Her raven-black hair was pulled back so tightly it looked like it hurt and was finished in a ponytail made immobile by what must have been handfuls of hair gel.

In a daily ritual, she would use her hips to push empty desks into a fortress around her desk, and then practically hissed when anyone approached. The week before, she stormed out of the room in quiet rage rather than work with the group of girls to which I'd assigned her.

"Why you beastin' us, mister?" Talia, the ringleader, had protested. "That ho Yvette don't work with nobody and we all like it that way."

I pleaded for respect and cooperation to no avail. "I hope no one ever talks about you like that, Talia."

"If they do, they'll walk out of here with less teeth, mister," she said.

"You are a real charmer, Talia. By the way, I have a name, other than just mister. It's Mister Boland."

"Whatever." She shrugged. My colleague Trey was so frustrated by the kids just calling him mister that he resorted to wearing one of those sticky name tags that read "Hello, My Name Is" and wrote in his last name. It still didn't work.

Then Nee-cole raised her hand. "I think that movie was really cool," she chirped. As happy as I was to have any kind of positive response, I knew she was going to catch hell for her comment, as she did for everything she said and did.

"What did you think was cool about it?" I asked.

Before she could get a word out, Talia piped up. "You think anything he puts up there is cool, you crusty-ass brownnoser."

Everything about Nee-cole broadcast that she was different and more innocent than her ninth-grade classmates: the petite frame, the pigtails, the timid walk. But what really gave her away were her curious but cowed brown eyes, ever magnified by a powerful set of glasses. In a school where seventh-grade girls had multiple tattoos and wore T-shirts that said "Gold Digger," "Hot Mama," or "I'm Not Easy But We Can Negotiate," Nee-cole wore the pink frilly clothes you'd see on a primary school girl. While most girls toted around makeup bags, she carried a cheap pencil case stuffed with a ruler, colored pens, and stickers. She was a teacher's good girl from the get-go, dutifully scribbling down everything I wrote on the board. She spoke without a trace of ghetto and paid the price for it from her peers.

"She like it cause it got white people in it and Nee-cole like anything white," Chantay added. That got an additional round of laughs.

The clock hit 3:00 p.m. The kids peeled out of the room with the jovial air of drunken friends leaving a comedy club. I apologized to Nee-cole, who sat staring blankly ahead.

"I don't know why they always say stuff like that to me," she replied.

"Ignore them, Nee-cole. You are just more mature than they are" was the best I could muster.

"Thanks for looking out for me, Mr. Boland. It means a lot." She was one of a few kids who used my name.

I skulked out of the building, purposely avoiding the coworkers who had been so encouraging about my lesson. I wasn't eager to share my awful results. My bike ride home, which usually energized me, left me nauseated. At the dining room table that night, Sam and I drank beers as we both worked. He was finalizing his script as production drew closer, and I was correcting the assignments on *Powers of Ten*. Aside from the usually obedient ten or twelve students, few kids had bothered to hand in anything at all, and when they did the page was only spotted with a few hastily written phrases. Then came the real surprise: Surly Yvette had actually written full sentences—lots of them. In an elegant script, she wrote, "I see the Earth, it is sparkling, blue, beautiful, and so far away. The solar system looks like the atoms and the atoms look like the solar system. It's all the same really. I know where those people on the blanket are, but where am I? This is an interesting movie." She ended with an urgent plea: *"PLEASE DON'T TELL ANYONE I WROTE THIS."*

I sat up, ramrod straight. The blur of my funk and the buzz of my beer evaporated. There was so much in that one freighted paragraph. She had let her defenses down and wanted to be seen as sensitive, intelligent, and aware. It was a faint vital sign: wounded, but not dead.

The morning after I showed the movie, I asked Tasneen, Yvette's eighth-grade reading teacher, about her. "It's a pretty bleak story. You sure you want to hear it? Sometimes it's better not to know."

I nodded, though I was unsure.

"In seventh grade, the kids were spreading rumors that Yvette was a slut. Then they started calling her a hooker. We tried to stop the harassment. We even called a class meeting about it, but nothing worked," she said. The lush cadence of Tasneen's voice made even tawdry high school gossip sound regal. "One day in class, I intercepted a note." She paused and sheepishly looked at the bottom of her mug of tea. "It said, 'Yvette blows old guys for a dollar under the Manhattan Bridge.' We punished the girl who wrote it for spreading lies, but she insisted it was true.

"Well, not long after that we were contacted by Child Protective Services. They weren't rumors. It was all true, even the stuff about the dollar. She was put into protective custody. We don't think she is doing it anymore, but she'll never outrun that story here. It's no wonder she doesn't trust anyone."

I tried not to act as shocked as I was. Even though my coworkers were sensitive and caring people, they would casually drop bombs like this and I would try to cover my greenness. You'd often overhear snippets like "Her parole officer was here yesterday...Yeah, seems like a lot of sophomore girls are living with their boyfriends...He's trying to scare up money for her second abortion."

My mind raced to understand. How could a child's life go so wrong, so haywire, so early? What parents would allow this to happen? Wasn't there anyone to protect her? I wasn't totally naive, I knew this kind of thing happened, but to a middle school girl?

The next day, I smiled at her as I handed back the papers at the end of class. I had written, "Yvette, your response is beautiful and thoughtful. You are an excellent writer and thinker. Thank you for sharing this. I promise not to tell anyone about your writing. I'd be happy to talk to you about it and anything else. Please come see me after class anytime." I made sure to put the paper facedown to show her that her secret was safe with me. "I'd like to talk to you about that more," I whispered. She glared at me, stuffed the paper into her backpack, and huffed out of the room.

The rest of the year, I never saw another sign, another opening, from Yvette. Every overture I made was stonewalled. I didn't reach her. I didn't save her. I hardly talked to her again. But I would never again look at the angry or blank stares of my students and think they told anything close to the whole story.

In November, on the night of the parent-teacher conferences, things went from bad to worse for Nee-cole. The hallway was packed with tense parents, some with clingy younger children in tow. Leaning against my doorjamb, I watched as the crowd made a sudden wide wake, the kind afforded only to those feared or honored. At the end of the hall, amid a sea of puffy black coats, I watched a riot of color slowly come into focus: a tattered orange vest, a tangle of scarves, rainbow leg warmers, and bootleg designer jeans. I couldn't stop staring. The statuesque woman drew closer, her dreadlocks interwoven with ribbons, shells, and the earphones of an aged Discman. She wheeled a suitcase behind her while keeping time with the tinny old-school music that pumped out from the earphones. I strained to hear. Was it Donna Summer's "MacArthur Park"?

As she got closer, I tried not to gawk at the unclear boundary between her forehead and hair. Covering a seriously receding hairline was a boxy, bruise-blue tattoo that took up much of her forehead. On the side of her face the tattoo continued with Josephine Baker–like pin curls permanently inked onto her skin.

She consulted a piece of paper, squinted up at my room number, and then looked at me. In a voice almost as theatrical as her appearance, she said, "Why, good evening, Mr. Boland, is it? I'm Charlotte Jenks, Nee-cole's mother. It's so nice to meet you." No other parent said it was so nice to meet me. She sized me up through the same bookish glasses her daughter wore and extended her hand. Her commanding posture and warm manner only added to my confusion.

I closed the door and she began, "I am not at liberty to fully explain the situation, but years ago circumstances forced us out of our home and I had to place Nee-cole in the foster care system. I love my child beyond words and am still very involved with her life. Her education is my priority."

"I see," I answered tentatively. I was in unfamiliar waters.

"I was unhappy with her middle school in Harlem. I did research and found out it was on the chancellor's list of underperforming schools. I had no choice. I pulled Nee-cole out and homeschooled her. But we didn't have a home so I made do and I taught her where I could, mostly on the subway, for the year." I restrained a gasp and nodded slowly.

She relayed more details without a hint of self-pity, but I wasn't absorbing much at that point. I felt nauseated and angry. How could such a thing happen in the richest city in the richest country in the world? And what to make of this woman. Should I admire her? Judge her sanity? Trust her story?

She went on to ask me questions about her daughter's progress, more incisively than any other parent had. At the end, she asked, "Are the kids treating her okay? We've had problems before with her being bullied."

I hesitated. Should I give it to her straight or spare her? "Oh, just fine. She's getting along with everyone." A mercy lie, but still a lie.

After that evening, word traveled like wildfire around the school. The kids were heartless. "Did you get a look at her? Mama look like a homeless clown. Yup, Nee-cole's mother is a HOBO!" Not just homeless, not just crazy, but a laughingstock, too; reduced to a word I thought was used only by people my grandmother's age. Other teachers and I tried to intervene, but our attention only widened the gap between her and her peers and made her even more of an outcast. Watching her suffer was even worse than what the kids were visiting on me.

Month after month, despite the cruelty, Nee-cole never seemed to give up hope of connecting. In December, her advisory unit had a Christmas gift exchange in the cafeteria. I sat a table or two away. She had saved her four-dollar-a-month allowance (the great beneficence of the foster care system) for offerings to the pack of nasty girls in her advisory group: a lumpy stuffed Christmas bear, sparkly lip gloss, a spiral notebook announcing, "You Rock!" (The stores in nearby Chinatown could turn even the poorest of the poor into gift-buyers.) She passed out the gifts, one by one, to a round of smirks and rolled eyes. Their ingratitude was run-of-the-mill, teen-girl cruelty, but still cruel.

Then Chantay got a cagey look on her face. "Oh yeah, we got you something, too." She handed Nee-cole a large manila envelope, which she eagerly tore into. Even at a distance from my faculty perch, I sensed it was a trap. Out fell a pile of magazine ads. Smiling but confused, Nee-cole spread the images out on the table, not understanding their vicious gist at first. I got it right away but wished I hadn't. Smiling fashion models had been horribly disfigured with blobs of purple eye shadow, mascara, and brown smears of foundation. The girls had re-created a hideous, cubist montage of Nee-cole's hobo mother with eerie accuracy. Nee-cole kept her frozen smile on, but I doubted it would last. All the girls laughed out loud, but most showed a shred of humanity by not looking at her after they humiliated her. But Talia, who was sitting across from Nee-cole, laughed right in her face. She laughed so hard she was falling off her stool. I started to make my way over to the table to give her hell and console Nee-cole, but I stopped cold. I felt so unhinged I thought I might do something reckless, violent, to Talia. I bolted out of the cafeteria, terrified to watch any more of Nee-cole's reaction and even more afraid of my own.

I stayed late that day, and by 6:00 p.m. just about everyone was gone. Only Jim, the janitor, remained. He was bald, mustached, and in his fifties, an utterly decent guy. With a few quiet uniform whooshes, he swept my room with an economy that comes only from twenty years of cleaning the same place. Without ever having seen me teach for even a minute, Jim could divine a lot from his decades of cleaning classrooms. He must have sensed my state. He pulled off his headphones and said, "Look, Ed. I can tell you aren't having an easy time of it. There's graffiti on the walls, candy wrappers on the floor, and the desks are kinda nutso at the end of every day. I live in this neighborhood and I know these kids got no goddamn respect for anybody. Just now, I had to change the toilet paper in the boys' bathroom because some punk soaked the whole roll with piss. Anyway, you're a good guy. I hope it gets better for you."

"Thanks. I appreciate that, Jim," I said, hoping to keep the uncomfortable conversation short. He closed the door behind him as he left.

If there was one thing I thought I knew how to do, it was to connect to people, even if we didn't share similar backgrounds. When I taught English in China after college, I was pretty comfortable being one of a handful of white people in a city of six million Chinese. While fund-raising at Barnard College, it wasn't unusual for me to be the only man at a reunion of two hundred women. During the height of the AIDS epidemic, despite my modest roots, I served as the gay fund-raising ambassador to the grand dames of the Upper East Side. But here I was at a total loss: Trying to connect with Yvette only drove her further away. Trying to connect with Nee-cole only got her more ostracized.

I put my elbows on the windowsill, my face in my hands. I winced thinking about everything Nee-cole and Yvette had endured. During the crisis with Kameron, I had fought hard not to cry as I stood in the bathroom stall. But here it was no use. I let go. At first I wept for their terrible lives, then their loneliness, and then for myself. I had never been much of a crier, and the tears in my palms seemed so unfamiliar, so out of place.

Scared by the intensity of my own reaction, I went outside for a breath of cold air and tried to snap myself out of it. I had a whole grade full of Yvettes and Nee-coles; some of them were even worse off than these two. How could I do my job *and* feel for their terrible lives? Being a whitey with a salvation complex was not going to help them. Maybe I was just too thin-skinned for this shit. But I knew one thing for sure: I didn't want to become so tough, so veteran, that I wasn't fazed by the thought of a seventh-grade hooker or a kid being homeschooled on a subway by her homeless mother.

I walked toward Delancey Street, where two little girls in braids with their grandmother were waiting on a worn green bench for the bus. The older girl was teaching the younger the rules of rock, paper, scissors. I stood there eavesdropping, hoping their innocent chatter would restore me, remind me how sweet childhood could be. I heard:

Paper covers rock.

Rock crushes scissors.

Scissors cut paper.

But there was no escaping the despair as I recited my own version quietly to myself:

Silence covers fear.

Fear crushes hope.

Hope cuts silence.

Chapter 6

Sweet Jesús

EVEN THE ROUGHEST boys would now and again show a chink in their armor and acknowledge your humanity in some modest way. It was always after school and usually with their girlfriends in tow. They might say, "Hey mister, you really like those white-people dough-nuts from that expensive place, don't you? No Dunkin' doh-dohs for you. I seen you chowin' 'em down in the teachers' lounge."

But not Jesús Alvarez; never Jesús. He was a shit—a perfect shit. He executed his role as a tormentor of adults seriously, almost pro-fessionally. Even mobsters I had read about were eager to show their warm and fuzzy side on occasion, but he was all business, all the time. A short, squat Puerto Rican kid, his mouth was permanently triangulated between a smirk, a snarl, and a wiseass smile. Even at fourteen, he had little black sprouts of back hair creeping out of his T-shirt. For a tough guy, he had remarkably long eyelashes. As if he weren't formidable enough on his own, his longtime girlfriend and coconspirator was the foulmouthed Chantay.

Jesús started his assault on me the first week of school, but it was indirect at first. Some kids said it was he who put Chantay up to her now-famous desktop defiance. He followed that up by furtively screaming trash talk into my classroom from the hallway while changing classes, "Bolan', who you ballin'? It ain't no chick."

I clearly recognized his voice (as if Beavis and Butt-Head had come up on the tough streets of the Lower East Side), but no matter how many times and ways I tried to catch him in the act, he was always gone, like an apparition.

He followed this trick up with a form of abuse by proxy, where he would home in on the more academic or earnest of students (or, really, anyone who showed the slightest sign of kindness toward me) and torture them in front of me. He alternated between sweet Neecole and brainy Byron, presenting me with a classroom version of *Sophie's Choice*. I tried to protect them both, to no avail.

Yet, his most infuriating trait was his ability to act like you simply didn't exist. Caught red-handed in some transgression—hocking a fat loogie onto Mexico on the class globe to show his disdain for its people or destroying a new textbook by creating a type of gummy worm carpaccio between the pages—he would simply stare through you with that "Did somebody just say something?" look on his face. No manner of rage or wit or pleading from me was ever registered. Even in my humiliation, I recognized his brilliance in these dark, naughty arts.

After about two months of this, I called Jesús's father to set up a meeting. Like almost every bit of advice I got from my coworkers, their take on just how advisable this was was split right down the middle. Half said, "Don't! It's the ultimate sign of surrender. The kids smell your desperation," while the other half proclaimed, "It's your only recourse. What's to lose?" One veteran, Marquis, recounted that the previous year, after he'd called the home of another tough student, the kid's mother showed up in the flesh in his class and beat her son for all to see. She had to be restrained by security guards.

At Sam's urging, I made one of my frequent early-evening phone calls to my sister Nora to help break the tie. "I've tried everything with this kid. Positive reinforcement. Befriending him. Being a hard-ass. He's been in the reflection room more than anybody," I said.

She was home cleaning up after dinner. Over the sounds of running water, clacking plates, and her daughter Millie practicing the recorder, she asked, "What the hell is a reflection room?"

"It's our euphemistically named detention center."

"No wonder the school is having trouble. What a dumb name. Maybe that's what we should start calling solitary confinement at the prison. The reflection room."

She continued. "I hate to break it to you, but ultimately, you need to realize that your students are people with free will. Just like you and me. You can do all you can, but in the end, it's not you who has the power over their behavior."

"I don't like that answer. Being powerless isn't fun."

"Welcome to their world. They have very little power in their lives, so they will use it where they can. Either of us would do the same."

She paused before going on, seeming to sense my need for reassurance more than truth. "Sure. Call the father. It doesn't sound like it could get much worse."

She ended the call with a strangely reassuring comment: "You know, in a weird way, you have it harder than I do. I can use real sticks and carrots with my kids at the prison that have direct consequences on the quality of their lives. But an afternoon in your reflection room sounds like a nice break for kids. You have it rough."

I hung up the phone and plunked down on the couch. I fantasized about Jesús being stripped of his beloved Air Jordans and Hollister hoodie and put in a pair of paper shoes and an orange jumpsuit.

About a half hour after dismissal, Jesús's father swaggered into my room for the meeting wearing a shiny windbreaker with some kind of International Brotherhood of Something union insignia on it. He was probably in his early thirties, but he looked young enough that he and Jesús could easily have been mistaken for brothers. Physically, they were carbon copies of each other. Jesús shifted uneasily at a desk in a corner. Without so much as a word from me, Mr. Alvarez planted himself at the desk immediately in front of Jesús, toe to toe, and launched right in.

"Jesús, this is a good school. People here like Mr. Boland care about you. He's a good teacher and an educated man. If they toss you out of here—and it looks like they might—you gonna end up in a place like Washington High."

"That's right," I echoed sternly.

Washington High was a notorious place. Bedlam with lots of gang violence. Three years earlier, rogue students had thrown a stool out of a fourth-story window, hitting a pregnant woman on the street who lost her baby and nearly died.

"You think you tough?" Jesús's father continued. "You a chicken-shit. You'd be begging the cops to take you home in the back of a patrol car from there." He laughed. "It would take you about a week before you'd get a buck fifty in your face."

"Yeah, Jesús, a buck fifty in your face," I said, repeating his comment like some kind of cooing backup singer. Then I realized I didn't have a clue what a "buck fifty" was. I later learned it's 150 stitches in the face from a razor attack. Handy information.

"You get yourself right, get an education, and show this man some respect," he went on.

Jesús tried to keep up the tough veneer, but I sensed something might be sinking in. He stuck out his chest, but he was silent for once. I was impressed, inspired, and at the same time ashamed of the subtle glee I was experiencing at seeing him on the ropes for the first time.

"Go stand in the hall," his father barked. Jesús walked out silently.

"I'm sorry about all this. I'm going through a real messy divorce with his mother. He and his brother are with me now, and it hasn't been easy for anyone. But that's no excuse. If he gives you any more lip, call me. Pronto."

"He's a good kid," I lied. "Thank you for backing me up. We just need to get him back on track." He locked eyes with me, shook my hand, and walked out the door.

I left that meeting brimming with confidence. Involving parents was key. Tough love was the answer. Jesús would turn; others would follow. The next day in class, he played it just right. He was an angel for the first fifty minutes of the period; at the end of class he created a small harmless scene. I guessed he didn't want to arouse the suspicion of his peers or Chantay that he was getting soft. But it was a détente I could live with.

The reprieve, however, lasted exactly one week, and then Jesús came out swinging again, seemingly worse than before. I called the father several times. I got a message or two back promising action, but nothing really changed after that.

The end of the semester was fast approaching, and the entire ninth-grade team was demoralized. We found it so alarming that a full third of our students were in danger of not passing ninth grade. Mei had just sent out letters to parents alerting them their child might not pass and urging them to set up a meeting. But only three parents called in response, one to say she was going to send a letter back saying we were crazy and didn't know how to teach her son.

In terms of discipline problems, I was getting the worst of it from the kids, but everyone was suffering. Bridget, the redheaded and wildly freckled science teacher, was also in the hot seat these days. She had taught in the backwaters of Laos for a few years, where kids would literally walk for miles barefoot to class, which was sometimes conducted outdoors. Many nearby children couldn't even afford the uniform that was required to attend the school. Teachers in Laos are generally revered, but as an American willing to come to the jungle, she had achieved near godlike status.

Her transition to Union Street was jarring, to say the least. She had a reputation as an excellent, meticulous teacher who ran a tight ship. Her tomboyish Peppermint Patty energy earned her both respect and disdain. When her requests that a boy pull up his sagging jeans to cover his crack or that a girl stop giving herself a pedicure in class were met with frothing rage and profanity, Bridget was incensed. It was baffling to many teachers that the disadvantaged kids we taught were, in an odd way, so spoiled. One day, after one indignity too many, Bridget flew into a rage about their ingratitude. She brought her fist down onto the overhead projector so hard she broke the damn thing and sent pieces flying everywhere.

My friend Porter, the ninth-grade English teacher, had a similar meltdown. During an advisory period not long before, he was chatting with Jesús and a group of boys when he mentioned his fiancée and their weekend plans. Jesús started laughing and asked, "Hey, do you ever flip her over and fuck her up the ass? You know, make her bite the pillow? That shit is tight!" Porter flew into an apoplectic rage. It was unsettling to hear such a usually mellow and kind-hearted guy bellowing down the hall after them. When he later came to my room, his mouth was still agape, his face beyond beet-red, almost an unearthly purple. Sprawled over a desk, he held his head in his hands and said, "Those little fuckers. I think I burst a blood vessel screaming at them so loud. I want to hurt that son of a bitch Jesús so bad. I want to slam him against the lockers." Like Bridget, he, too, had taught abroad in the third world and was utterly revered as a Peace Corps volunteer in Madagascar. The only disturbance he encountered in two years of teaching there was when a six-year-old girl showed up obliviously wearing a T-shirt from a Western charity drive that read, "I'm shy but I have a big dick." When someone translated it, her older brother raged against the class for laughing at her, but his outburst was short-lived. He showed up the next day proudly wearing the shirt, only too happy to share its message.

At our ninth-grade team meeting on a cold January afternoon, we passed around a tin of stale Christmas cookies and, in desperation, formulated a triage plan. Dorothy, the petite blond math teacher who seemed to have a relatively easy time with the kids, had an idea: "If we all agreed to teach one more period every day, we could significantly decrease the size of each class from about thirty-two to twenty-five. Smaller groups would be easier to manage. We could split up some of the cliques that are giving us the most trouble. More learning would get done." It was a great idea, and I was proud to be on a team that was ready to innovate instead of just bitch and moan.

We brought our restructuring idea to Mei. From the dismal first-quarter grades and harrowing daily discipline log, she knew the ninth grade was in a bad way and appreciated our initiative. She ran the idea by the instructional superintendent for the district and got back to us quickly with approval. The new semester would start in three weeks, which gave us time to plan carefully for the transition. The whole ninth-grade team was reenergized by the idea. The final step was to get the blessing of the UFT, the teachers union.

The role the union played at Union Street was far more sane and professional than it had been at Eugene Debs. There, teachers were forever quoting "the contract" as a way to do less and less. The amount of required teaching time per day was dictated down to a thirty-second interval. Faculty meetings were not to exceed forty minutes, according to the contract. Watching the clock like hawks, most of the teachers were packed up at thirty-nine minutes and out the door at forty minutes on the dot, even if the vice principal was in midsentence. (If a kid ever did the same in their classrooms, they would have had a fit.)

Even worse, I watched the union rally around a teacher who had supposedly been assaulted by a student. In reality, a nasty kid had abruptly yanked some papers out of her hand and she didn't think he had been punished enough. She claimed her wrist was seriously injured. It quickly turned into a farce of hearings, arbitrations, doctors' reports, and interviews of a dozen student witnesses. She missed whole days of class as a result. She went around the faculty room showing her supposedly injured wrist in some kind of air-cast from a ninety-nine-cent store, but there was clearly nothing wrong with her.

I expected better from the younger, more dedicated faculty at Union Street, and, by and large, I found it. The relationship between faculty and administration was far more cooperative and professional. Both sides were more interested in the welfare of the students. Until now.

In response to our request, our union rep, Seth, the sophomore math teacher, convened a meeting with the ninth-grade team the following week, where he announced, "Well, guys, I heard back from our district rep. I'm sorry to say, we can't go forward with your plan. The contract clearly says we teach six hours and twenty minutes, followed by a thirty-seven-and-a-half-minute student help period every day. Your plan exceeds that by quite a bit."

"But we are *electing* to do this. It will help the kids and us," fumed Bridget.

"If management sees that teachers are willing to work more without more compensation, they'll hold that against us during the next round of negotiations," Seth said.

"It's an idea from teachers, not a demand from management," added Dorothy.

"I'm sorry, but that's just the way it is. We have to adhere to the contract strictly or the whole thing falls apart."

"The whole thing *is* falling apart, and by that I mean the ninth grade," I sputtered. We trudged out of the room. We lost, and the kids lost; the union and its beloved contract won.

As the new semester started at the end of January, a wave of unexpected violence gripped the area immediately outside the school. Escalating gang rivalries were blamed. Cops started to stand at the corner of the school during dismissal. Chatter in the hallways placed Jesús at the center of much of the trouble. It somehow involved his parents' ugly divorce and possibly a new girlfriend from the wrong gang. I overheard otherwise in the little snippets in the hallway: "No, it was about the drugs. *Siempre los drogas.*" "No, it's a project-against-project thing, dumb ass."

While all this talk swirled around me, I looked out my window to see a pair of construction cranes whirring about a sleek, rapidly ascending high-end condo. I had just read about an apartment on nearby Avenue D selling for $4 million. Hot yoga studios, boutique hotels, and mescal bars rubbed shoulders with bodegas, ninety-nine-cent stores, and public housing. I wondered if the influx of investment bankers who were buying these seven-figure apartments knew—or cared—what was happening a mere three blocks way. They wouldn't have to worry about local schools, of course: Forty thousand dollars in annual private school tuition could make that problem go away.

I got a taste of the trouble myself after school one day. I'd stopped in a corner bodega to buy a sleeve of Oreos for the kids in my study group. As I left the store, I heard a woman yelling, "I'm sick of you punks and I'm calling the cops." Underneath some nearby scaffolding was a middle-aged mother with a baby carriage, getting in the face of one of the "corner kids," who acted as lookouts for gangs, as she called the police. The thug in question pulled out his phone and pointed it at her. Without much emotion, he said, "Go on, dial it, bitch, and watch what happens to you and your kid. I'mma send this pic to all my niggas right now. We'll find what floor you live on." Her face froze, she snapped her phone shut, and she walked away pushing the stroller.

A week later, I was leaving school when I saw Mei on the street frantically shouting into a walkie-talkie. Three cops were on the opposite corner. A gang fight had broken out right outside our building but dispersed as soon as the police arrived. Teachers and students alike knew it would just get played out someplace else close, but where? Just as I started biking home, I saw two kids hop a fence into a deserted parking lot behind a CVS pharmacy. I circled around the block and found an entrance to the lot. Without warning, I found myself on the edge of a real live gang fight. True to my gay roots, my only point of reference for such things was the rumble scene in *West Side Story*, but I was now seasoned enough not to expect the Sondheim/Bernstein/Robbins version.

I was conspicuous to say the least: white, middle-aged, clad in khakis, and wearing a space-age bike helmet atop my beat-up Raleigh Racer. As I rolled onto the scene with all the street cred of Mary Poppins, two groups of fifteen kids each were hurling threats back and forth. A few small skirmishes were being played out on the margins, and then a brutal fight began between two guys in their early twenties. As I was fumbling for my phone in my backpack, some kids recognized me. I heard my name called from somewhere. There was a throb in my temples. I felt strangely embarrassed, as if I'd pulled open the door of a bathroom stall on someone.

As I looked down at my phone to dial 911, I heard a voice I didn't recognize. "If you're smart, mister, you'll stay out of this. It's none a your fuckin' business." I looked up and saw Theo, an obese seventeen-year-old freshman, drug dealer by trade, who had come to school a grand total of two and a half days that year. I ignored him and called 911 and then Mei.

I scanned the crowd and saw Jesús's brother, a junior at Union Street, and finally Jesús himself. No surprise there. I tried to lock eyes with Jesús to let him know I was wise to him, but he was too busy to notice me.

Searching for more faces of my students, I came across a slightly older man in a denim jacket in the middle of the crowd. He seemed out of place among the kids. As the fight escalated, he jeered and pumped his forearm, shouting, "That's it, Nelson, show that punk-ass bitch who's boss. Whale his ass." I inhaled hard and looked down as it hit me: It was Jesús's father.

He was as convincing there as he was in my classroom. "Pop that bitch in the face; pop him." So much for fatherly concern. Whoever Nelson was, he was inspired by the orders. He now had his bloodied opponent on the ground and delivered a coup de grâce with a power kick to the stomach. I'd been fooled and was angry at myself for being taken in so easily before by Mr. Alvarez's hollow talk and cheap theatrics.

As quickly as the melee started, and without any obvious explanation, it dissolved. The two sides walked off throwing insults over their shoulders. Two older boys helped the bloody and hobbling kid walk away. Several Union Street kids passed by me without so much as a glance. Invisible again. I stayed for a while waiting for the cops, but none came. The next morning I recounted the story to Marquis, a veteran history teacher with experience on both coasts. "Treachery from teenagers, that we can expect, but parents? Come on," I seethed. "And then the cops; why didn't they come?"

"There were no weapons. They're not going to bother with that shit." Marquis sighed. "And you know what? As crazy as it sounds to us, that father may be trying to teach his son to survive in a hostile environment the only way he knows how. It's easy for us to say, 'Violence isn't the answer,' because for us it's not, but that isn't an option for a lot of kids outside these walls." I was just looking for someone to share my outrage, but instead I got another dose of uncomfortable, confounding reality.

Until then, I hadn't given much thought to the landscape outside of school. But a quick and unhappy checklist formed in my head as I walked down the hall: The cops don't care. The union doesn't care. The rich neighbors don't care. The parents don't care. Who was in this fight with us? I couldn't help but feel like a sucker.

The following month brought Teacher Appreciation Week. Standing at my mailbox in the teachers' room at the end of day, I smiled as I read colorful notes covered with cartoon stickers from the usual suspects, mostly good girls like Nee-cole and smart boys like middle-class Lucas and Norman, the wheezing asthmatic I was so very protective of because I feared he would die in my class. He gave me a coffee mug filled with Hershey's kisses. I knew that the mug (and the note taped to it) was really from his mother, but I appreciated it nonetheless. But there was another note, this one on a ripped piece of notebook paper, with handwriting that was large, cursive, and clear. Having seen so little of it, I didn't recognize Jesús's handwriting at first: "Dear Mr. Boland, thank you for never giving up on me. Jesús."

I stared down at the card. In resignation, in sadness, and with what little anger I could still muster, I said to myself in a low voice that hardly seemed my own, "Dear Jesús, I am trying hard not to give up on you and everyone else here." Even three months before, I would have seen this note as an ember of hope. Now, I couldn't help but wonder if it was his conniving father or his manipulative girlfriend who had put him up to this. I tossed it into the wastebasket and started to walk out of the lounge.

I thought I was forgiving. I thought I was understanding. I thought I was mature. But, so quickly into this experience I began to loathe my students, resenting everything about them that was their lot—their poverty, their ignorance, their arrogance. Everything I was hoping, at first, to change. I was supposed to be the adult, but I had to check myself repeatedly as childish resentments and judgments flared up over petty things like Mariah's body odor, Lu Huang's single four-inch strand of facial hair, or Nestor's disgusting bag of *chicharrones*. And now treating Jesús's gesture with such contempt.

Hoping it would save me from my own cynicism, I pulled the note out of the trash and crammed it into the bottom of my backpack.

CHAPTER 7

Lord Byron

"Sam, are you awake?" I asked into the darkness. The only trace of light in our bedroom came from the cryptic green flashes of the computer modem.

I was hoping to conceal the twinge of fear in my voice, even from Sam, who was curled up next to me. I stroked the silky black hair on his forearm, secretly hoping he would stir and comfort me, but he was out cold. He was in the throes of editing his film and was as stressed and exhausted as I was.

I used to boast to friends that no matter what my troubles, I could always do three things: eat with gusto, get an erection when called for (and even, at times, when it was not), and sleep like a log. As my first year in teaching wore on, each of these constants crashed and burned.

In pretty short order, I lost my appetite and dropped twelve pounds. In the sack, I half-flaccidly and halfheartedly went through the motions of lovemaking with poor Sam, while a tape of horrible classroom scenes looped in my brain. And, like most mornings, here I was two hours before the 6:30 alarm, fighting off alternating fits of self-pity, guilt, and fear.

I had always been the upbeat cheerleader in my pod of friends.

From my cheery perch over the years, I had watched a host of friends spiral into depression from terrible breakups, job troubles, or illness. Now it was my turn. Whatever encouraging words or gestures I had extended to them must have seemed as unhelpful and hollow as the ones they were lately offering me. That particular morning, two faces haunted my predawn jag: the brilliant Byron and the rigid vice principal, Gretchen. I was failing them both in very different ways.

From the minute he crossed the threshold of my classroom, it was clear that Byron was a prodigy, even if his intellect was shrouded under serious mumbling and a heavy Jamaican accent. The first week of class, when Byron softly announced where he was from, he was teased by classmates with the predictable jokes about dreadlocks, ganja, and Bob Marley. Byron was the antithesis of all these things. With tightly cropped hair, an air of utter sobriety, and no trace of reggae bounce in his step, he was an old soul at fourteen. He wore the same tattered black hoodie every day, which only added to his monk-like aura.

One early September afternoon, he wandered into my classroom and without a word started perusing my bookshelf, skipping over the kid stuff and pulling out my graduate school books. He flipped through a half-dozen of them before he spoke a word.

Without making eye contact, he asked, "Why do you think the Indus Valley river civilizations disappeared, Mr. Boland?" and a little bit later: "Why is Sweden so well suited to socialism?" In the course of the first semester, the kid sent me scrambling to the Internet and the teacher's edition of the textbook on more occasions than I could count. He was exactly the kind of kid I was hoping to help, and this was perhaps in part because I saw much of my young self in him. The bookshelf scene in particular brought me back to sixth grade when I stayed after school to administer a world history test of my own making to my beloved teacher Miss Hilderbrant (which, to my great joy, she failed).

Byron visited me after school often and gradually started to open up to me. His young life was defined by missed opportunity. Uprooted from a good school in Jamaica while in middle school, he immigrated illegally to the States with his single mother and moved to the run-down town of Port Chester (known colloquially as "Poor Chester") in Westchester County.

There, his mother worked as an assistant in a law firm, where stories of her brilliant son trickled up to the boss's office. Her boss was a trustee of the Larchmont Academy, a prestigious private school that did a great job with the Project Advance kids who were placed there. Byron applied and was awarded a full scholarship, one that he would never use. Constant relocation is a curse of the poor, and Byron and his mom unexpectedly moved to the Bed-Stuy neighborhood of Brooklyn. Maybe the circumstances were too ugly to convey or maybe they thought it was none of my business, but I could never get a straight answer out of him (or his mother) as to why they moved.

While sharing a bag of Skittles with Byron after school one day, I learned about another terrible misstep. "Last spring, I was admitted to Stuyvesant, but I decided to come here to Union Street instead," he said with pride, thinking I would applaud the decision. Instead, I was horrified.

Stuyvesant High School was probably the most selective public school in the nation, the training ground for Nobel laureates, attorneys general, and titans of business. Typically, about 29,000 kids apply for just under 1,000 spots in the freshman class. In recent years, the school has admitted as few as seven black students (not 7 percent but a total of seven black kids) into its freshman class.

"I'm curious. What made you enroll here?" I asked, concealing my shock that he had squandered yet another golden ticket.

"My mother and I thought Stuyvesant was too big. We knew I would get a lot more attention here, and we liked the international studies aspect."

I could see how Union Street must have sounded so nurturing, with only ninety students in a grade. Its cheery website pledged to prepare students for the best colleges in the country while immersing them in an international curriculum. The school taught Mandarin, offered trips abroad, and boasted that its faculty members had lived in twenty different countries. Even gym class promised global flair, offering cricket and rugby, instead of the usual basketball and volleyball. Little did Byron and his mother know, it was really another struggling inner-city school with a well-designed website and a fresh coat of paint.

Having come from Project Advance, I felt a special responsibility to help this kid. So about three months into school, I sat him down. "Byron, we need to have an utterly candid discussion." There was no need to dumb down my vocabulary with this kid. "We are accomplishing next to nothing in my class. A lot is happening, of course, but very little of it involves learning." He shifted his skinny frame awkwardly in a desk that was covered with obscenities—most of them about me. "From now on, I'm going to give you the *New York Times* to read every day. When you are done with your classwork, and let's be honest, it usually takes you about five minutes, make a list of questions from the articles you have read and we can discuss them after school. I can also get you books on any topic that you like. And we need to find you a challenging summer program. I know you must be bored and frustrated. I'm sorry. I wish I had a better handle on classroom discipline for both our sakes."

Byron picked at some of the newly sprouted fuzz on his chin.

He seemed ill at ease and embarrassed for me. He wasn't used to a teacher confessing gross incompetence to him. What high school freshman was?

"That's very considerate of you to think of me. Thank you," he mumbled.

The next month, Byron's mother, a warm, animated woman with a serious dose of Caribbean rectitude, came for her parent-teacher conference. Big-boned and dressed in office wear, she exchanged pleasantries with me in a way very few parents did. Once we were behind closed doors, I didn't mince words. "Mrs. Williams, I know this may sound unusual coming from a teacher here, but I am telling you, in confidence, that you should consider having Byron transfer to a different school."

"Really? But this is so much better than the middle school he attended. That was so chaotic, he would come home with migraines. There seem to be a lot of caring teachers here."

"There are great teachers here, no doubt, but Byron needs to be around more kids who are just as smart and motivated as he is. I'm afraid he won't be well prepared for college." Her mouth turned into a pout, still unconvinced. I locked eyes with her for emphasis. "I used to work for a program for gifted students, so I know what he's missing. Trust me. I can help you find a better school."

She looked at me with apprehension while saying, "Okay... well... we'll think about it."

"Also, please don't mention to anyone else here that I suggested this. Schools don't like to lose high performers like Byron." This woman was used to nonstop praise about her son in meetings like this. Telling her she was doing a disservice to her son by keeping him here made her uncomfortable.

"I appreciate your concern," she said, but she seemed happy to leave.

*   *   *

The same November morning that I gave Byron his first *New York Times*, I spied the vice principal, Gretchen, in the teachers' lounge. Mei had just announced a change in reporting: All the ninth-grade teachers would now answer to Gretchen.

As she did every morning, Gretchen was logging student offenses from the previous day onto a whiteboard in colored markers: "Jaden, 11th grade, defiance; Naylani, 9th grade, profanity; Malik, 10th grade, texting in class." In one of her many tributes to the East, she finished by drawing a pair of lotuses on either side of the list of crimes. She turned to me and said sternly, "I need to talk to you."

At first glance, Gretchen was the hippest-looking person you'd ever seen working in an educational institution. She sported a soft, graying Mohawk, funky rectangular glasses, and dozens of hammered silver bangles that went halfway up her thin arm. Every time she bent one way or another, she revealed another arty tattoo: an ankh here, a labrys there, some kind of mystic eye of god winking at you from her shallow cleavage. Her office was overflowing with exotic Eastern musical instruments that I didn't know how to pick up, much less play. When she wasn't citing the Bhagwan, she was quoting the Buddha.

Once I woke up and smelled the incense, however, I realized Gretchen was a study in cognitive dissonance. Despite the Woodstock veneer, she was much closer to a Victorian schoolmarm. Liver-lipped righteousness never looked so cool.

Every week, I left my supervision meetings repeating the "edujargon" she spouted, often without explanation. I would walk out of her office pep-talking myself, mumbling the argot she used, hoping it would work its magic. "Yes, Gretchen's right, I must 'chunk' the curriculum and 'scaffold' their learning." While she was probably an excellent teacher herself and had an impressive command of educational theory, she imparted little useful advice or encouragement, at least to me. And even though we were both gay and about the same age, I couldn't find a shred of common ground with her.

The rest of the faculty was split down the middle on their feelings about Gretchen. Some admired the seismic jolts of fear she could inspire in some of the toughest students. But most grew tired of her tales of how perfectly everything worked at the school she had cofounded and worked in until the previous year. "Well, at Brooklyn Arts Academy, what we did was...Do you know what worked great at Brooklyn Arts?"

Not long after receiving a scathing evaluation from Gretchen, Patrick, a history teacher in the middle school, was scavenging for a snack in the teachers' lounge refrigerator and asked us aloud, "If she created such a fucking educational paradise over there at Brooklyn Arts, can somebody tell me why she left so quickly?"

In the teachers' room that morning, after she finished writing up the final infractions on the discipline board, Gretchen pulled me aside. "We are overdue in scheduling your first formal classroom observation." I dutifully set down a stack of *Economist* articles I had photocopied for Byron and pulled out my planner.

Observations were a big deal, especially for new teachers. Receiving tenure depended heavily on the formal observations administrators conducted over the first three years, and if you got tenure, you basically had job security for life. Thanks to the powerful teachers union, the UFT, it was next to impossible to fire a teacher in New York City with tenure. (In 2009 and 2010, despite widespread student failure, only *three* of the fifty-five thousand teachers with tenure in New York City were fired.) Case in point: A principal walked into a primary school classroom where the teacher was asleep and apparently drunk. She was relegated to one of the famous "rubber rooms," where teachers in trouble wait, sometimes for years, for an arbitration panel to decide their fate, all the while collecting full salaries. But even the sleeping/drunk teacher later returned to the classroom. And a high school music teacher in Queens, who had confessed to sexually harassing students, collected $1 million in salary (plus benefits and pension) over a period of thirteen years spent sitting in the rubber room while appealing his case. While these are rare and extreme examples, they certainly reflect a terribly broken system.

As usual, I was eager to keep my conversation with Gretchen short, so I hastily scheduled a time for her to observe me. But as I was closing my planner, I had the sinking realization that I had invited her to see my by far most disruptive class. But it was too late; the die had been cast.

Over the next week, I planned with great care and came up with a lesson I called "Cracking the Code of Egyptian Hieroglyphics." It involved a short textbook reading, projected photos of an obelisk, and a simple translation handout. Over coffee one morning, I ran my lesson plan by Monica and she blessed it as pedagogically sound. "It's creative and engaging. Accessible, but with high-level content. And it's smart to have something so visual given their literacy levels." I then shared my fears about my classroom management.

With a titter, she reassured me: "Don't sweat it. The kids aren't going to act out. Especially not in front of Gretchen. They're terrified of her." I felt a world of relief, and as I walked out of her room I said to myself, *Monica is the true Buddha spouting wisdom, forget that withholding sphinx Gretchen.* For the first time in weeks, I slept well that weekend before the big day.

The day of the observation arrived. The kids burst into the room, amped up after lunch as always. I had plenty to be nervous about anyway, but a third cup of coffee had really set me on edge. I turned the projector on and the lights off. Gretchen slipped in the back, at first unnoticed by the kids in the dark, and began furiously scribbling notes.

"Hey, what's that freaky Ms. Dufour doin' here?" someone wondered out loud.

"She here to see if he can teach," another voice clarified.

I projected my first slide: a hieroglyph of a duck. It inspired a quick, lone quack in the darkness and a laugh in response. I reprimanded on cue. Others joined in and soon there was a flock. The "vice principal effect" that Monica had promised did not materialize. A group of boys in the back row playfully slapped one another's heads. The frenzy fed off itself. My escalating threats fell on deaf ears. Soon the kids were all but swinging from the lights. The Tic Tac tucked in my cheek was melting fast, and I could smell my own acrid breath. Knowing I had to get through the lesson, I pushed on.

Even during the escalating mayhem, Byron was dutifully taking notes, as if he were a scholar at the British Library. There was nothing to be learned; what *was* he writing down?

Suddenly, the lights went back on. I looked to the back of the room, expecting to find some kid pulling a prank. Instead, I saw Gretchen charging toward me. Through clenched teeth, she asked in a low voice, "Don't you see how they are behaving? The disruption? The profanity? I am formally canceling this observation and doing an intervention." She was practically twitching with rage. I looked down and spied a crumpled lunch bag on the floor. I wanted to crouch down and breathe into it to stave off hyperventilation.

Then she turned to the students. "The way you are conducting yourselves is a disgrace." She squinted down at a Post-it. "Braithwaite, Palacios, Epperson, Vasquez, Sanders, Woods. Go immediately to the office, call your parents, and tell them to get in first thing tomorrow to see me. Am I being absolutely clear?"

The rogue students filed out, shoving desks out of their way and cursing under their breath. They were followed by Gretchen, who left with a memorable parting shot, growled under her breath: "I used to teach juvenile delinquents in Vermont who had huffed half their brains out on glue. *They* acted better than this. In my twenty years in education, I've never had to cancel an observation. This is the *worst one I have ever conducted.*"

After she was gone, the room settled into an eerie quiet.

In a bizarre twist, I was suddenly presented with my dream classroom scenario. The monsters had been removed and I had a roomful of kids eager to learn. Among them were the dutiful and respiratorially challenged Norman, earnest Bradley, middle-class Lucas, and ever-loyal Nee-cole. And of course Byron, who was still tracking me with his stoic expression, interrupted only by the robotic pulse of his eyelashes. I stood there numb.

I had been pretty good, or at least decent—and certainly passable—at just about everything I had ever tried in my life: I could look back on rave reviews for a tiny soliloquy I gave in the first-grade play, a promotion to head altar boy, glowing performance reviews at various jobs, a powerful volleyball serve, and a much-praised ability to whip up with ease gumbo, or porchetta, or Thai curry. Before this, I had powered my way largely unscathed through a terrible gay starter marriage, the worst days of the AIDS epidemic, and the nasty diva-driven politics of Lincoln Center, but here suddenly I was depressed and ashamed, undone by a bunch of thuggy teenagers.

Sure, I was god-awful at math, spelling, crafts, and any kind of choreographed dancing, but not the "worst ever." "Bad" or "terrible" would have been enough to send me reeling, but "worst ever" had never seemed in the realm of the possible. Until now.

I knew I needed to rally. I turned back to the work sheet. In a blur,

I asked someone to try to decipher the hieroglyphics. Naturally, Byron raised his hand.

His voice was deep and serious for a fourteen-year-old: "There are both pictographs and ideographs here. And I am reading it from right to left." He paused. "So, I think that line says, 'The man is a scribe.'"

I tried to focus on his answer, which was of course right on the money, but I could only register a heaving sense of shame. I stared at the jumble of symbols on the board in front of me: falcons, asps, ankhs. Now they only reminded me of Gretchen and her lousy tattoos. I slowly turned to the board, reasonably sure Byron had the translation right, but I could read only one message no matter how I looked at it: "Worst ever."

Still in a daze from my botched evaluation, I careened into the faculty room and plopped down in "the chair."

No one knew where the upholstered leather, midcentury modern chair had come from, but it clearly had a story. Chairs like this didn't just magically appear in the teachers' lounge. It sure hadn't come from the Department of Education, whose standard-issue furniture looked like it could give you tetanus just from sitting on it. But whatever its origins, it had been placed next to the copy machine and become the place of refuge for teachers in distress. Often the rookies and sometimes even the veterans would stagger into the room, looking shell-shocked and lost, and plop down in that cozy chair.

Invariably, one of the more compassionate and experienced folks on staff would perform a little visual triage on the troubled soul, put down the *New York Times* or look up from their computer screen and say, "Everything all right?"

I must have appeared in a really bad way that day, because I got

a full-court press of love and support. First, the middle school reading teacher and faculty spirit bunny Rebecca immediately came over
and silently gave me a hug and patted my head. Then my rock Monica sat on the armrest and quietly shared the story of a tough former
NYC cop who taught at Union Street the year before. He, too, had
turned to teaching in middle age and everyone assumed he would
have no problem with classroom discipline, given his experience.
But his background turned out to be his Achilles' heel. The kids
didn't care in the slightest that he had been a cop, and he had no
capacity for disrespect of any kind. Late in the year, a boy spit on
him and he resigned. I was relieved to hear it and, at the same time,
ashamed at how comforting I found the story of someone else's humiliation.

The last period of the day ended and more teachers straggled
into the lounge. Spontaneously, a group ritual of solidarity
unfolded as we consulted the great unwritten cosmology of reasons for classes gone wrong. The collective wisdom sounded like
this:

"Well, naturally. It was first period. Of course they didn't get it.
They're basically still asleep. There is research that shows teenagers
literally can't think until 10:30 a.m. It's a fact."

"Obviously, it was last period, they'd lost their focus. Don't sweat it."

"The kids are always off the chain before lunch. They're starving,
and pent up."

"After lunch, forget it. They're in an altered state. They are all
jacked up on Coke, gummy bears, and MSG. Then they go to the
yard and whale on each other for a half hour. What did you expect?"

This, in effect, offered an excuse for every failed class period. The
other newbies and I drew on this canon liberally and it gave us great
comfort. These excuses could be supplemented by seasonal varia-
tions:

"Winter is basically a collective depression. Haven't you heard of seasonal affective disorder? Kids get it too."

"It's spring; the kids are way too hormonal and horny to think."

Then things really got absurd: "It's not the rain that makes them hyper, it's the relative humidity. Really." I half expected to see a teacher pull out tarot cards or chicken entrails to explain it all.

Tired of relying on these excuses and still reeling from my disastrous observation, I decided the key was really all in the lesson plans, and I vowed to use the horrible textbook less and my own materials more. But when I wrote my own lessons, which was a huge time commitment, the results were hit-or-miss. I had the kids create Myspace pages for Frozen Fritz, an intact Copper Age ice mummy found in the Italian Alps in 1991. I had them make their own mini-textbooks on Greece that we would send to a needy school in Africa I'd found online. At first these projects gripped their attention, but as soon as the fun and theatrics ended and real effort was demanded, they lost interest. Whole weekends disappeared in planning, only to be spit back at me in minutes by the kids on Monday morning as "borin'" or "This is mad stoop-id, son!"

I was trying everything I could to make the ancient world come alive for them. We were studying ancient Rome at the time, and despite my showing some liberal doses of the popular movie *Gladiator* to pique their interest, the kids were really not feeling it. On the subway home, with a lesson on Roman law to prepare that evening, I read an article about the rapper Lil' Kim's recent release from prison. On a whim, I mashed the two together and emerged with: "Would Lil' Kim have received justice under the Roman system of law?" I shortened a lengthy CNN web article about the trial of the popular rap star whose posse was involved in a shootout in the lobby of a radio station. I replaced all the words they'd have trouble recognizing with simpler ones and made a cheat sheet about

Roman justice, introducing terms like "trial by jury" and "edict." I researched her songs to find a hit without explicit content to warm up the kids (no mean feat).

On a Friday morning, I played a clip from her big hit "No Time" as the kids strolled in.

"Mister, stop actin' like you down with hip-hop! Come on, man. You frontin'," commented the ever-insightful Fat Clovis.

"Clovis, if I thought it would get you interested in history, I would rap the entire lesson."

"Please, please, please, don't do that. Anything but that," he begged me. For once, we could both laugh at the same thing and it felt great.

I announced the lesson and passed out the materials. The room was strangely quiet while they looked them over, followed by an unprecedented fifteen minutes of silent reading. Without much prompting, they took out pencils and pens and started writing on the work sheets. Something was terribly wrong. What was going on?

I was so ready for the usual chaos, so prepared for the sudden wrenching reversal, but that moment never came. Almost everyone filled out an answer sheet, even Jesús. There was something resembling a real discussion. To my great joy, Chantay used the term "self-incrimination." It was glorious.

I was sure I was the subject of some cruel secret experiment engineered by the chancellor of New York City's schools. Was the mayor in the hallway looking in? Was it a giant practical joke hatched over lunch? *Hey, let's fuck with Mr. Boland's head and actually learn something today.*

What had happened? Teacher taught and students learned, that's what happened. If nothing else good came of that year, at least I had my one delicious day with Lil' Kim and the kids.

I was so overjoyed and energized that I sped home recklessly on my bike. I immediately plunged into planning for the next day as I told Sam of my great victory. "It worked, baby. Like a charm," I said as we sat on the living room floor folding warm laundry into piles. Giddy with my success, I had another idea for a lesson and scoured the website of the Vatican Museum and dug up my old Latin textbook. When the lesson was finished, it seemed just as good as, maybe even better than, the Lil' Kim one: understanding daily life in Rome through graffiti. My opening example was a doorway in the ancient city of Ephesus covered with graffiti that translated to "Eat at Joe's" and "Stop pissing here!"

I tried to conceal my enthusiasm the next day as I explained the lesson. The ever-sassy Jaylisa Ortega (whose parents, I later learned, were named Jay and Lisa) sauntered into the room late, a dramatic entrance surely timed to show off her new tinted sunglasses and pink velour tracksuit. Before she sat down, she scanned the work sheet on her desk and shouted, "Hey, what you doin', Mr. Boland, trying to make this shit interesting for ghetto kids?" It wasn't quite the success of Lil' Kim, but it was solid. For the first time all year, I thought, if the chancellor observed my class today, he would not have me arrested. And that was a sign of progress.

To celebrate my victory, my coworkers treated me to a raucous, tequila-infused happy hour at our usual dive bar in the East Village. Dancing to a Lil' Kim song on the jukebox, I waved the work sheets in front of them that showed traces of learning from some of our most difficult kids.

My phone buzzed with a call from Sam. I could barely hear him over the din of the crowd. "Meet me on the corner of Houston and First in a half hour." I weaved my way to the spot, and there he was with a bunch of floppy orange deli tulips and a wide smile.

"Tonight, we are going to a restaurant we can no longer afford," he announced proudly. He squired me over to Prune, one of our favorite places in the city.

Over a plate of buttery sweetbreads, he toasted me with a Moscow mule: "It sounds like you are starting to turn it around, baby." I looked down, almost afraid to acknowledge any progress. There had been so many false victories. He squeezed my hand over the table and whispered as if it were a spell, "You'll do it, you'll do it, you'll do it. If anyone can do it, you will."

Chapter 8

Free Freddy!

Learning-disabled. Middle school. Boys. Those three categories, taken together, are the trifecta of all difficult teaching assignments. The prevailing wisdom was, if you could teach them, you could teach anybody. Fittingly, a saintly lame-legged man named Wilson filled that purgatorial post at the Union Street School. Balding, droopy-eyed, and with a waxy look of permanent patience, he bore an uncanny resemblance to a statue of Saint Joseph and was said to work miracles with his troubled charges.

My brief reprieve with successful lessons on Lil' Kim and Roman graffiti was short-lived. For no clear reason, the following week things were back to their chaotic status quo. Several people, from Mei the principal to Jim the janitor, told me I should go observe Wilson in action. "Most of your kids with serious behavioral problems have underlying learning issues. If you can figure out how to reach them, everybody else will fall into place," added Monica.

In December, I choked down my pride and timidly poked my head into the middle school Special Education room during one of my free periods. It was the decrepit old band room that had been commandeered when there was no more money for a music program. Wilson was quietly orbiting around a small, antsy circle of about ten boys and a bored-looking teaching assistant.

116

I recognized several faces from my required weekly stints of supervising the reflection room: I saw Eric, the boy who had pleasured himself—to completion—in the back row of a language arts class. A pair of skinny twins who had brawled against each other in a legendary hallway fight; they inspired the oft-repeated teachers' lounge joke, "Who won? Who can tell?"

But the most famous of all was Calvin, a tiny twelve-year-old Chinese American boy with severe autism and an unfortunate penchant for playing with his asshole—scratch-and-sniff style—in public. He also had an encyclopedic command of the New York City transit system, having committed the entire subway map, corresponding bus transfers, and maintenance advisories to memory. Given any request, he would look upward for a fraction of a second and then spit out an itinerary in an eerie, robotic-sounding formula. He was much sought after by teachers before field trips.

If this job was good for one thing, it was reversing racial stereotypes. Anyone who ever bought into the "Asians as model minority" myth should visit Union Street. Gloria Lin could throw blood vessel–bursting fits with the best of them. She once stormed out of my classroom with this memorable exit line: "I hate you. I hate this fuckin' place. I stink at school and I'm glad I do." Tze Han, a recent emigrant from Fujian Province, was a member of a notorious neighborhood Triad gang, said to be involved in human trafficking and other organized crime. He often came to school escorted by a truant officer. At least he came to school. Angus Zhao lived in the apartment directly opposite my classroom; it was so close I could literally see what herbs his mother was growing on her kitchen windowsill. He never came to school, not for a single day of ninth grade.

★　　★　　★

As predicted, everything I observed in Wilson's classroom was organized, positive, and focused on learning. There were clearly systems
and rules in place, but it didn't feel overly rigid. I was surprised,
however, by one glaring flaw. His "para" (a paraprofessional who
serves as a teacher's assistant in classes with high-needs kids)
seemed totally checked out. Sitting in the circle with the kids, he
was doing next to nothing. I probed a little further while the kids
read silently.

"And what role does your para play here?" I asked, striving to put
on my most professional educator voice.

"I don't have a para this period," Wilson responded.

"Who's that, then?" I asked, hiding my finger behind a notebook
as I pointed toward the young man.

"Oh, Freddy? Oh, no. He's not a TA. He's a student." He chuckled.

"Really? That kid's in middle school? He looks like he could be in
his twenties."

"Well, yeah, he's probably close to sixteen by now. Let's just say
he has serious family issues, low skills, and a chronic attendance
problem."

I observed Wilson for the next hour, noting his every word and
gesture. After class, I peppered him with questions, all the while trying to sound like I knew what I was talking about. He winced as
I tossed out, and then mangled, the Special Ed argot I had learned
in one half of a graduate school course dedicated to the subject:
dyslexia, ADD/ADHD, "the spectrum," individualized education
plans, processing issues.

With a wave of his hand, saintly Wilson dismissed all I had said.
"Forget all those labels. Forget those techniques. The key is to forge
a genuine relationship with the kids. They'll find a way to learn, a
way to behave, but they have to trust you and know that you care
about them."

"But is that enough? Their problems seem so different, so big. How do you remediate for them all at once?"

"Build the connection and the respect. Start small, with little victories. Soon, they'll start to really work for you—and for themselves." On reflection, Monica and Nora had said much the same thing. I was hoping for specific reading techniques for kids with dyslexia, some easy shortcuts; instead, I walked away with a dose of loving folk wisdom. Another unexpected discovery, but, as usual, so much harder and more time-consuming to put into practice.

I climbed the stairs back to my room even more befuddled. Plain old teaching was hard enough, but when you added Special Ed students to the mix, matters got really confusing. Even the term itself seemed an impossibly wide catchall, including emotional, behavioral, physical, and developmental disabilities: the introverted girl who had trouble reading; the boy with MS in a wheelchair; a gifted, highly medicated kid incapable of sitting still. All Special Ed.

I sat down at my desk and pulled out my list of Special Ed students and their diagnoses. As I scanned it, I was reminded of another conundrum. Many kids in the grade with the most obvious disabilities weren't officially labeled "Special Ed." Having students evaluated was a long, expensive, bureaucratic process. While parents knew their child would get extra services, they rightly feared the stigma attached to the label. And they didn't want their child warehoused with kids who had much bigger issues. And, finally, some parents were just too overwhelmed, unfamiliar, or neglectful to go through the process.

Even more maddening, I knew from personal experience that, as usual, things seemed to be different for the rich. I knew plenty of upper-middle-class families who had kids with learning disabilities, some very serious. One wealthy and superbly educated couple I know had a son, Adam, who attended an exclusive private boys' school in New York. Despite everyone's best efforts, he could barely recognize his letters in first grade. The school and the family blitzed the problem in quick succession with evaluation, diagnosis, and services. They hit hard and early. Fast-forward twenty years: He went to Princeton and is now at Yale Law School. I can think of at least five other similar situations with children of well-off families. For them it seemed like a temporary setback, but for most low-income students, a diagnosis was more often than not an educational life sentence of never-ending catch-up. I thought back to Nora's prison classroom filled with eighteen-year-olds struggling, with quivering lips, to pronounce the word *though*.

I marched down the hall to the main office and pulled out the folders of my Special Ed students. Each had state-mandated, specially developed education plans, some as thick as phone books. Some had been diagnosed and given services for eight or nine years. In primary school, they usually had smaller classes with learning specialists, resource rooms, and one-on-one tutoring. At Union Street, most of the high school Special Ed students were in mainstream classes, but had Special Ed teachers who traveled with them from class to class to offer additional support in many but not all of their classes. They had yearly mandatory progress meetings with parents and specialists. And yet, for all that effort, many still struggled to read at a sixth-grade level. Were the services they were getting *that* inadequate or did their life circumstances play an even greater role than the diagnoses themselves? Why were they so hard to help? It was surely some combination of these factors, but what was really at the root of the problem? In frustration, I slammed the rickety file drawer shut.

I had turned these questions over and over in my head for months, but that afternoon I came back to a blind spot: What about me? How had I so conveniently forgotten my own early learning problems? Although I was never formally diagnosed, I had surely had signs of a learning disability as a child. Not only was I among the worst readers in my first-grade class at the Sacred Heart School, but I was also so distracted and scattered that I had a hard time finishing my work.

I thought back to a fall afternoon in 1970, when Sister Concepta called me to her desk rather sternly. I'd never been summoned there before. From the first day of school, I had adored Sister Concepta, and she, me. She was big on manners and respect, and I gave her both in abundance. I also made her laugh, particularly when I kept asking her what a "concepta" was.

Sister looked at me in a way I wasn't used to. Exaggerated by the square frame of her black-and-white veil, her gaze was intense and her nose pointy. She was the kind of modern nun who wore a simple veil, but she had been liberated from the starched wimple and other medieval trappings of the older generation. Mind you, she wasn't as radical as a "pantsuit nun," those rebels who shed all the traditional trappings except for a small cross on their lapels, but she was at least in the twentieth century.

"Eddie, I'm worried that you aren't finishing your assignments," she said, pulling out a sheaf of barely completed, purple mimeographed work sheets. I loved those sheets for their strong, pleasant gasoline-like vapor. I'd cradle them in my palms and quietly huff them, even before I knew what a buzz was.

"What are these?" she asked, pointing to the circles I'd drawn around my answers. Each had a network of spouts, portals, and chimneys built into it.

I told the truth. "Those are the airholes for the right answers. I didn't want the words to suffocate inside the circles." I thought she would appreciate my thoughtfulness, but she narrowed her eyes with concern.

"And what are these squiggles?" She tapped a pencil on another sheet with crude geometric shapes inside the circles.

"That's, um, food and some furniture so the words are cozy." I swallowed hard, and my Adam's apple pushed on the top of my plaid clip-on tie.

"That's nice that you are so concerned about the words, dear, but you have to focus and finish your work."

"Okay." I felt my expression grow pouty and grave. Even then, I knew what I was doing was weird and felt a sudden stirring of shame. I returned to my little, worn wooden desk, so old it had a hole where an inkwell once was.

Not long after, Sister Concepta called my parents to an after-school conference. After a short while in the hall, I was brought in. Kindly and quietly, she told me we needed to work on my reading. Every day at 10:00 a.m., she would look at me and touch her watch. It was our secret signal for me to go across the hall and work with Sister Kathleen at a little table. Sister Concepta made it sound like an honor or a treat, and I bought it. She was getting me the help I needed. I don't remember much of what we did at that table, but toward the end of the year, Sister Kathleen said I no longer needed to come visit her.

I shared more with many of my struggling students than I first realized. I was just lucky enough that the right people intervened when they did.

In January, about a month after my visit to Wilson's room, Mei pulled me aside during my free period. She was always smiling, so it was hard to know if she would be sharing good news or bad. "Freddy is going to be promoted from the seventh to the ninth grade."

"Freddy, from Wilson's class? Don't tell me that kid managed to meet grade requirements."

"No. I wish." She snickered. "It's just that he's sixteen now and getting ridiculously old to be in middle school. He's outgrowing those little desks in the Special Education room. He'll start with you on Monday, if he chooses to grace us with his presence that day. Good luck with him." Unlike the hard-ass Gretchen, Mei had an inimitable way of presenting bad news and near-impossible challenges with such optimism and humor that it always softened the blow.

"I can't wait to have another young scholar join our ranks," I said, trying to match her good cheer.

I announced to the second-period class that Freddy would be starting with us the next day.

"Freddy? Man, that kid is *old*. He's too hairy to be a freshman. He's got hair everywhere," Fat Clovis blurted out. Ninth-grade boys cherished every wisp of facial hair, every spiky whisker, and they enviously noted any growth on others.

"Everybody, please make an effort to welcome him," I said.

As soon as I turned my back, someone added matter-of-factly, "Yeah. Be nice to that hairy criminal or he will *fuck you up*."

I was quickly learning not to ignore comments like that. Gossip, jokes, and even slander held important clues about what might be going on with students, so right away I launched into a fact-finding mission. Even by tough public school standards, Freddy had been dealt a rank-bad hand: a father who was nowhere in sight; a mother in the Bronx projects with serious diabetes; and an older brother, a gangbanger, who was imprisoned on Rikers Island for running a drug ring. Freddy had joined the family business and been arrested for dealing himself. The family's housing situation was in serious jeopardy because of laws designed to evict convicted drug dealers from public housing. He was the sole breadwinner in the house.

Freddy was in court not long before the start of the school year. When a judge offered him a year at Rikers or three years of probation, Freddy said he would take Rikers. In all his years on the bench, the judge had never had anyone take that option before and responded, "Son, do you know what a rhetorical question is?" Freddy shook his head no. The judge declined the kid's request and gave him probation.

Given Freddy's reputation and confirmed criminal record, I was afraid to have him in my class. The last thing I needed was another problem child, and this one sounded epic. My fears, it turned out, were unfounded. This kid, on the rare occasions when he showed up, was a peach. He rarely spoke to me or anybody else. For most of the period, he would just stare forward. He had the tear-shaped, maudlin eyes of a stuffed animal that belied his stormy life. He would politely take my work sheets and hand them back to me an hour later—without so much as his name on them. But, hey, he didn't cause any problems. Given what he had seen, I suppose that spitballs and back talk to teachers seemed childish to him, not worth his time or energy.

Could I blame the kid for being so checked out? He had way more serious adult problems than I ever did. By the time he was sixteen, he was a small business owner, breadwinner, and near convict. I felt silly giving him work sheets on the Han dynasty.

About two weeks into his transfer to high school, Freddy's cell phone spit out a loud, jarring hip-hop ringtone in my class, and, adding to that already serious offense, he pulled the phone out of his baggy jeans and answered it. I charged toward his desk and launched into my usual diatribe about the ban on phones and the corrosive effects of electronics on one's education. As I was bellowing, however, I was carefully monitoring his reaction. Given his history, I was not eager to find this kid's boiling point.

"Mister, please, let me take this," he implored. It was the first time I heard him speak a whole, audible sentence.

"Freddy, I can't imagine that call is more important than your education," I said, borrowing that sappy line from some other teacher.

He paused and said something in rapid-fire Spanish into the receiver.

"It's my brother, calling from Rikers. It's the only call he gets this month. I miss him and really want to talk to him. Please, mister." He spoke softly.

This bit of information turned the head of every kid within earshot. They were eager to see what I would do. I pulled Freddy into the hallway. I thought of Wilson's advice about building trust instead of just following the rules. At the same time, I didn't want to set a bad example if I let him take the call. My mind was racing. I heard the crash of a desk being overturned in my room. His brother was repeating Freddy's name on the crackling cell phone he held in his palm.

I took a gamble. Playing the heavy wasn't working anyway. Why not try something else? "Look, Freddy. Let's be clear: I am not giving you permission to talk on your cell phone." His face dropped. "But I am giving you permission to go into that stairwell for five minutes and do what you need to do."

His face surged with surprise. He wasn't big on emotion, and his glee echoed inside me.

"Thank you, mister," he said as he walked to the stairwell.

I charged back into class and tried to play tough to the crowd. "Freddy is on his way to the principal's office. Does anyone else have a pressing call they need to take?"

Ten minutes later, Freddy returned to class and gave me a quick, furtive grin. I had never seen him smile. Another first. I kept on my stone face and nodded to him. At the end of the period, he handed me a work sheet on world religions with actual writing on it. Until that point, I wasn't really sure he could write at all. True, he had blatantly grafted whole sentences about Zoroastrianism from the textbook onto the questions about Buddhism, but it was something, a beginning. As I tucked his sheet into a manila folder, I smiled, thinking about one of Wilson's adages: "Start small and build on the little victories."

"Nice work, Freddy," I said. He smiled shyly again as he walked out the door.

"If this keeps up, I might actually be able to help this kid," I told Sam at home as he taped Freddy's assignment on the fridge as a sign of hope. I called my sister Nora and told her the story, thrilled to have a victory to share with her instead of my usual dirge.

I returned the next day, but Freddy was nowhere to be seen. For weeks afterward, Freddy simply disappeared.

During our next ninth-grade team meeting the following month, Sita the social worker made a special appearance in my classroom. Her normally friendly tone was grave.

"Guys, I'm sorry to come in unannounced, but we have a very serious issue. Does anyone know anything about Freddy making calls during school hours? His probation officer came by yesterday and he was furious. It looks like Freddy may have been making calls for his brother's drug ring on our watch. It's gotta stop or we are going to be in some deep shit."

My eyes slid slowly down toward my notebook and I started to formulate a confession, a lie, some way to dig myself out of another shit heap. I knew they could easily figure out that at least one call had taken place during my class. A few seconds passed and her question turned into a general admonition: "Please, everybody. We don't need this kind of attention. No more calls for Freddy during class." She paused, and a wave of resignation seemed to overcome her sense of alarm. "Of course, that is, if the kid ever shows up at school again."

She walked out of the room. The rest of the team gathered up books, transparencies for overhead projectors, and piles of homework, and filed out to the teachers' lounge for lunch. I usually would have joined them, but I stayed behind for a tuna sandwich and some self-pity. The normally chaotic room was silent. I swallowed hard and brushed some crumbs from my shirt. I was no Sister Concepta, and even the wisdom of the saintly Wilson had failed me.

CHAPTER 9

My Funny Valentina

ONE AFTERNOON IN the middle of February, with about ten minutes left in the day, my classroom door swung open and a girl I had never seen before sauntered in. She had the jaunty, hunched swagger of a prizefighter and an attitude to match. "Here," she said, tossing some papers onto my desk with a blasé flick of the wrist. All attention immediately went to the new girl. Even Nestor and Blanca, the love-birds whose eyes were always locked and fingers interlaced, took the time to look up and notice her.

She had a high, sassy ponytail, an oversize nose ring, and, most noticeable, an epic derriere showcased in a pair of acid-washed jeans carried with ostensible pride. Her T-shirt was emblazoned with the flag of one of the smaller Caribbean islands.

I squinted down at the papers. "Everyone, please welcome Valentina." New students often just showed up without warning, sent by Margie, the beleaguered main office assistant. Who could blame her? She was more triage nurse than secretary, sorting through a sea of barfing, beat-up, and asthmatic students, enraged parents, and pissed-off teachers bothering her about direct-deposit problems on payday.

As she made her way to an empty desk, Valentina's new class-mates greeted her with a long string of moos and oinks. If this were a prison movie (and at times, it felt like it was), this would have been the scene where the newcomer is paraded in front of the cellblock, jeered at by the old-timers. But this newbie was giving as good as she got.

"Step down, all y'all niggas, or I'll stab you in your neck. Don't get me tight, bitches." Her script was spot-on, but the voice was all wrong. She spoke with a high, wet lisp that utterly undermined her street cred. All thirty kids laughed at once. I tried to rein in the chaos, but happily the class ended before it got worse.

After school, Gretchen explained to me that Valentina was a "safety transfer," a prime example of a Department of Education euphemism. Supposedly, the term meant the removal of a student from a school because his or her safety was at risk, but here it meant a compulsive brawler who wreaked such havoc that she had to be removed from her school—stat.

The next day, Valentina entered class, late again, and peered through the darkened room at the image I had projected on a screen, the *Dogon Couple*, a famous sixteenth-century African sculpture of a pair of seated royalty from Mali. She pulled out a ridiculous large pink pen with a pom-pom on top of it and got right to work on the handout I had prepared. In contrast to nearly all her peers, she wrote in complete sentences, in handwriting that bordered on the baroque. A true romantic, her *i*'s were dotted with small hearts. Over her shoulder, I read her comments, snarky but on the money: "Well, isn't it obvious that they are a couple? His hand *is* on her titty. I bet they are rich and important. The way they sit is regal." *Regal?* That kind of vocabulary sure set her apart. Only Byron, who was scribbling out his usual tome, outdid her.

"Nice work," I whispered over her shoulder. She smiled and batted her eyelashes but then quickly resumed her default "Don't fuck with me" face.

Most of her classmates struggled with even the most basic questions. Not confident enough to use pens, they eked out simple fragments in pencil, scarred with red eraser marks: "a man ~n~ some lady siting," wrote Blanca. "They mad skiny people" was all Nestor could get down. Ashamed, many shielded their work from me inside their curled arms.

Done with the assignment, Valentina quickly became bored and started to exact revenge for the previous day's unfriendly reception. She started on Norman: "What you looking at, you crossed-eyed piece of shit? Nigga, those frames ain't even from LensCrafters, they from Medicaid!" Then she turned to Dannisha: "Did they give you that nice book bag at the shelter, honey? You fat black bitch."

By this point, I had become so desensitized to the words *nigga* and *bitch*, they seemed like just another form of the third person singular. I checked my amusement at the way she dismantled them all and tried to break up the trash talk, to no avail. "Valentina, I need to see you after class," I said over the salvo of insults.

Once everyone else had tromped out of the room, I perched on a desk next to her. I was trying to move past my usual, ineffective "shame on you" lectures, which didn't seem to work anyway, and tried a more honest approach.

"Well, Valentina, one thing is clear. You sure like to get into it with your classmates."

"You saw they was provokin' me, didn't you?" she shot back. *Provoking!* Again, I was loving her vocabulary.

"Don't worry, you got them back pretty good. But forget that. I know something that they don't. I read what you wrote in class about the sculpture. It was very insightful and well written. You can't fool me. I can tell from just that one sheet of paper that you have a very fine mind." Her face went deadpan; she may have even been embarrassed. "If you choose to turn that mind on, you will really go places. But all this fooling around will get you nowhere. I can help you develop that mind, but it's your choice."

She shook her head and rolled her eyes. "Sure, anything you say, mister."

The more I observed Valentina, the less I could figure her out. One afternoon, I watched as two male security guards were barely able to restrain her during a major brawl with another girl, while a string of venom poured out of her mouth. The next day, she was outside school on a nearby park bench caressing and cooing at Moose, her brindled miniature dachshund, like a first grader.

About a week later, Sita pulled me aside after a faculty meeting. Early on in the school year, she and I had bonded over our dislike of Gretchen. And just that day, we had spent our lunch break doubled over, mocking her New Age approach to education. "Better learning through crystals and Reiki!" we joked. But just two hours later, Sita looked sheepish and grave.

"We have an issue. Valentina has filed an incident report accusing you of sexually harassing her."

I laughed. "Jeez, between being a full-time faggot and sexually harassing girls, you wonder how I find the time to teach."

"No, I am serious and this is serious." She took a deep breath. "Of course, I don't think it's true, but I have no choice but to investigate the situation and alert Gretchen and Mei. I'm sorry, but I am mandated to." I laughed again, but this time it belied a growing blast of panic.

Because I was the subject of the investigation, I wasn't privy to many of its details, but I knew that Mei and Gretchen were taking statements and interviewing students. After about a week, a hearing of sorts was assembled. Sita; Valentina's adviser, Katy; Gretchen; and I sat in a circle in my classroom. I was a seething mix of pissed-off and scared. The last time I remembered feeling like this was in eighth grade when, as head altar boy, I was wrongly accused (but ultimately acquitted) of pocketing collection plate money. Sita read quietly from a report: "Valentina states that a week ago Thursday, after fourth period, you kept her after class, got very close to her and said, 'You are mighty fine, you turn me on, and I can tell you like fooling around.'"

"Let me be clear. I did not and never would say those words to a student. That's absurd," I stammered, my face growing hot. "I told her she had a fine *mind*, which she needed to turn on, and to *stop* fooling around."

Innocent as I was, I also felt a stinging, displaced sense of guilt. There were plenty of shortcomings that I could have, and really should have, been called on the carpet for. Gretchen was directly facing my desk, where a tower of uncorrected homework had grown so high it threatened to topple over. It was next to a binder full of sloppy half-completed lesson plans. The desks were scarred with graffiti, the floor littered with a day's worth of projectiles. No one was learning anything, but I was getting nailed for this bullshit?

I suspected that nobody really thought I was guilty, but the exercise in bureaucratic ass-covering dragged on nonetheless. Gretchen had the final word: "To protect you both, we will institute the following rules: You are never to be alone with Valentina. Don't violate her personal space. And refrain from using any language that could be misunderstood as sexual. You need to choose your words very carefully when you speak to children. Nothing will go in your file at this time." Her tone was so condescending she might as well have come over and patted me on the head.

Then I had a queasy revelation: This was almost the same panel of judges that had condemned Kameron Shields, aka Nemesis, after he defended himself for his empty threat to blow up the school. A few months ago, sitting in the exact same circle, I could live with the fact that a bad kid got sent away for saying something he really wasn't going to do because he was guilty of myriad other crimes. Now I was in the hot seat and filled with similar indignation. What a scary rabbit hole I'd fallen down. My situation and that poor kid's were far more parallel than I wanted to admit—both of us guilty but charged with the wrong crime. And in the time-honored American tradition, the brown kid did the hard time while the white man got a slap on the wrist.

A week passed and again I took a seat next to Sita at the sticky white lunch table in the teachers' room. We had barely spoken to each other since the hearing.

"Sita, I want to clear the air about the situation with Valentina. Off the record, what do you think was behind it?" I asked. She shifted uneasily in her chair, but I pressed on: "Did she really believe I was hitting on her? Or was it just a power play on her part? Am I giving off some creepy vibe I don't realize?"

She spoke just above a hush, eager to keep the conversation private. "No, you don't have a creepy vibe. It's so hard to know what is going on with that kid. She's from a seriously screwed-up family. God only knows what she's been exposed to at home. Abuse is rampant. Honestly, I think she has a crush on you and just acted out in a twisted way."

"What? A crush? No way."

"These girls had very few male teachers in elementary school. Most don't have any adult men in their lives at all. You are a nice-looking guy and you paid attention to her. Besides, didn't you ever have a crush on a teacher?"

"No." I took a spoonful of chili from my Tupperware.

Her voice started to rise. "But you were surrounded by a loving, middle-class family. And that was an age of innocence compared to now. Come on. Don't you see the way these kids are growing up here?" She looked as frustrated as I was.

I shot back, "But we can't just explain away someone's horrible behavior because they have had a tough upbringing. It doesn't do them—or us—any good." I was suddenly sounding far more right-wing than I wanted to and it started to make me sick to my stomach.

Exasperated, I went back to the computer room for my free period and started to prepare lessons for the unit on India, pulling up a series of web pages from different sources. Each one of them seemed to have the same damn picture of the Taj Mahal. I spent an inexplicably long time staring at one of those photos.

In an instant, I was taken back to 1978 and my first day of high school. I was in search of my Afro-Asian Social Studies class. In a daze, I wandered into room 217 and set eyes on Mr. DeFazio. My lust was instant, powerful, and ineluctable. A college football stud, John DeFazio was broad and darkly handsome, with wolverine-like levels of body hair. There was no better foil for my five feet of hairless prepubescence; his olive oil to my soda bread. In grammar school I had been taught by sexless nuns and single women. I hadn't expected this. I shifted inside my new-for-school brown polyester pants and prayed that no one saw my erection.

It soon became apparent that Mr. DeFazio favored the football players and wrestlers that he coached; his indifference to me was total. So early in the year I set out to impress him with an academic tour de force. I poured my heart and soul into the first research paper he assigned on a World History topic of our choosing. I thought long and hard and settled on the Taj Mahal. Just as Shah Jahan had constructed that famous alabaster slab as a loving tribute to his wife, so my meticulously researched paper would be a valentine to Mr. DeFazio.

I even took the trouble to go to the main branch of the Rochester Public Library to unearth facts and features that would surely dazzle him. Did John (yes, we were now on a first-name basis in my imagination) know that Shah Jahan planned to build an all-black version of the Taj for himself directly opposite the white one? Or that the building was called "a teardrop on the cheek of eternity" by a poet?

I pumped precious dimes with abandon into a loud, orange Xerox machine, trying to frame each image just so. There were close-up pictures of the facade's delicate tracery and a map of greater Agra. The night before I handed the paper in, I lay in the bathtub, staring at the ceiling, tugging on my scrotum and envisioning the waves of praise and attention to come.

A few agonizing weeks later, Mr. DeFazio handed back the papers. I knew it was going to be a special day, because he wore a short-sleeved shirt that showed his hairy, muscled guns. I flipped through the pages, eager to interpret every comment. But there were none. Not one. Only a solitary B on the last page, red but bloodless. I walked out of the room feigning indifference but collapsing inside.

Over lunch the next day, against my better social judgment, I sat with the geeks from the honors section of DeFazio's class. I carried my Taj paper on top of my books like a distress sign, a lovesick badge. Between bites of Underwood deviled ham, my brilliant cousin Tom looked down on it and impassively told me that in giving instructions to his class about the term paper, Mr. DeFazio said, "Somebody in the other class did their paper on the Taj Mahal. Don't do it on something stupid like that."

I laughed out loud in the student computer room thinking about it. It seemed so ridiculous in retrospect, but at age fourteen those impulses were potent and painfully real. Repression, peer pressure, and a puritanical school culture kept me well in check, but Valentina and her peers had far fewer barriers to hold them back from running wild. They were almost reckless with their emotions and budding sexuality. Sita knew what she was talking about.

Burned by Valentina and left vulnerable by the administration, I followed orders and kept my distance from her after the hearing. She treated me with a mix of mild disdain and detachment. From afar, I watched as she used her bag of tricks on others throughout the school year.

"Hey mister, gimme a dollar," Valentina would shout in her weird little-girl voice to anyone who would listen, in the hallways, in the middle of a test, to oblivious old men on the street during field trips. One afternoon, escorted by Mei, a highly decorated Iraq War veteran visited our class. Expecting to be hailed like Caesar, instead he got, "Hey mister, gimme a dollar." The class roared at his flustered response.

A pair of Special Education experts, two middle-aged women who looked like they had just tumbled out of a Talbots catalog, inspected my class one day. They paced up and down the aisles reviewing the work of my students with learning disabilities. I was surprised by how much time they spent talking in hushed tones to Valentina, who had no diagnosis that I knew of. Afterward, they peppered me with questions: Why wasn't she on the Special Ed roster? Had I reviewed her IEP—the federally mandated plan that all Special Education students must have on file? Hadn't I seen the classic signs of her dyslexia? I fumbled, obfuscated, and lied my way through the conversation. With a condescending smile, the older inspector told me, "Because you realize, of course, the school would be in violation of federal law if she wasn't given reasonable accommodations." Sensing another Valentina-generated shitstorm on the horizon, I tracked her down in the hall at dismissal and asked why she hadn't told Ms. Hancock, her adviser, or me about her dyslexia.

She tittered, "What? You think I'm a retard? Oh no, mister, I'm not Special Ed. Don't get me tight. I was jus' fuckin' with that lady's head, but I did like her shoes." I exhaled. My shoulders dropped and I turned away without saying a word. Walking back up the steps, I was secretly gleeful to know that she could play the experts just as well as she could play me. I probably should have reported this transgression, but the less I had to do with her, the better off I would be.

Another morning the following week, after I'd confiscated a cell phone from Chivonne, one of Valentina's friends, I intercepted this pithy message sent at about 10:00 a.m.: "Hey gurl, gonna go to school today, but first i gotta smoke this blunt all the way to my face, take my lil' Moose for a walk, and get some pictures developed. C U soon!"

I called the aunt who was raising Valentina to discuss her poor attendance and erratic classwork. When I finally got through to her, she seemed shocked that Valentina was disruptive. "Really, sir? My Valentina?" she said in a thick Caribbean accent. "But she's such a shy girl, a lonely girl." I hung up the phone, even more puzzled than before. Who was this kid?

In the spring, I noticed that Valentina had become the center of attention of a group of skinny sophomore boys, most of them recent emigrants from Africa. Leaning against my doorjamb, I watched them follow her up and down the halls, laughing, talking dirty, and calling her name—a great white shark with a school of pilot fish in tow.

"Yo, Valentina, we havin' a lil' par-tee at Mamadou's house tonight and you is da guest of 'onor," said one boy with a lilting Cameroonian accent.

"Fuck off. You all just trying to get with me." She scanned his physique and let her eyes land on the baggy jeans he was swimming in. "I need a man who can give me a meal, not some skinny boy with a snack." This drew howls from everyone within earshot.

"Don't you worry. We'll fill you up, bay-bee," responded a member of the boy chorus.

Not long after, I gave a test on ancient Greece with the essay question: "Describe three contributions that American society today has inherited from the ancient Greeks."

Valentina's response was perplexing and unique as always: "Women in ancient Greece was treated just like meat. They had to cook and clean and have sex whenever the guys wanted to. Anyway, now a days, it's just the same, guys go around gassing gurlz heads up, telling you that you's beautiful and shit. After a while, you give in and get with them. But, BAM! Then they're gone and you're no good to them anymore."

Whatever the correct pedagogical response to this was, it sure wasn't covered in graduate school. I wasn't touching this one. I wanted to tell Sita or Valentina's adviser Katy, but then thought better of mentioning anything sexual about her to anyone. To protect myself, I chose to ignore a cry for help.

When spring came, it brought the much-awaited class trip to Six Flags Great Adventure. Somehow, Dorothy, the math teacher, had persuaded Mei that a sham promotional event billed as "Math and Physics Day" at the amusement park could be counted as an academic field trip. We prepared for weeks: coordinating payment plans, gathering permission slips, making threats to leave kids behind at school if their behavior didn't improve. They talked incessantly about the deep-fried onion "blossoms," the bumper cars, and, most of all, the Kingda Ka, the world's fastest and tallest roller coaster.

The big day arrived. As our class burst into the park, we passed by another school group, obviously from the suburbs. Surrounded by a sea of blondes and near blondes, a middle-aged teacher in a navy polo shirt had drawn a complex diagram of a roller coaster on a whiteboard, annotated with terms like "vector" and "g-force." They had taken Math and Physics Day to heart, while our kids, who struggled all year with basic algebra, ran by heckling them.

The ninth grade dispersed throughout the park and I sat silently on a bench for a half hour holding my face up to the sun, the peace interrupted only by the whoosh of nearby rides and distant joyous screams. I was calmer and happier than I'd been in a very long time. But soon a pack of Union Street girls found my hideaway and announced that they were headed to Kingda Ka.

"Man up, mister, and get on the Kingda Ka with us," Chantay urged.

"Come on, mister," said Talia, carrying a giant soda in one hand, with a bowl of Dippin' Dots in another and a big pretzel hooked on her pinky.

"You always tellin' us to push ourselves; well, go over there with us and push yourself a little," Valentina added.

They got the better of my pride, and I found myself waiting in line for the ride in a ridiculous faux-jungle setting. In a maze of metal dividers, dire signs warned us every ten feet of the dangers of the ride to anyone pregnant, short, or with a heart condition, which caused a flurry of jokes about who was knocked up. Over and over, we watched as the teeming carloads of kids dropped straight down forty-five stories. After an hour, we finally loaded in. My buddy Porter, who had also been roped in by the kids, sat next to me. As the ride climbed, the air was still and the kids were silent. The car paused at the apex for a second. Suddenly, it plunged. The downward force was so great I couldn't even close my eyes. A thin line of drool was pulled out of my mouth and spread across my cheek. My body tightened so fiercely that I inadvertently butt-dialed Sam on my cell phone and he got a two-minute message of nothing but teen screams. I remember nothing but white, blank terror. As I staggered toward the exit, the ride attendants were hawking grainy pictures of us all on the ride in mid-fall.

"Nobody back at school gonna believe you had the nuts to go on this ride, mister; you better buy that picture," Chantay advised.

"I'll buy it if you try to clear up your bad case of potty mouth," I replied.

"Deal," she said in between speedy chews of a wad of gum.

She was right. On the bus ride home, I watched with a jumble of pride and embarrassment as the kids passed the picture around and praised me for my valor. Valentina, looking peaked and unusually subdued, just rolled her eyes and passed the photo on.

After the field trip, Valentina disappeared for more than a week without explanation. On the day she finally returned to school, Katy, Valentina's adviser, walked into our ninth-grade faculty meeting late, looking ashen and with her mouth slightly agape.

"Everything okay, Katy?" Dorothy asked.

"You're not going to believe this. Valentina just pulled me aside at dismissal and said 'Hey Miss Hancock, you wanna know something that you don't wanna know?' By now, I thought I had heard it all from that kid so I said, 'Sure, lay it on me.' Valentina got a weird grimace on her face and said, 'Well, you know that Kingda Ka is the world's fastest roller coaster. I went on it twice. On the bus ride home, I started bleeding mad bad and had to go to the hospital. Well, that sure took care of it. Now, there's no more baby. That's that.'"

"My God. Really? Did anyone know she was pregnant?" asked

Dorothy. A series of soft gasps went up and then uneasy silence. The meeting went on; I sat there numbly turning the details of the story around and around: Of course she knew she was pregnant. Wasn't that what she was trying to tell me in her crazy essay on ancient Greece? In the roller-coaster line, she saw those signs warning about pregnancy. The girls had even made jokes about it. I was sure she had done it intentionally. Yes, she was young, poor, neglected, but anyone knows better than that. Didn't she know what a risk to her health it was? And, I was no right-to-lifer, but didn't she have any conscience? No remorse for aborting her pregnancy on a roller coaster? And then to act so damn glib about it. Monster!

But that night, as I feverishly recounted it all to Sam over dinner, my snap judgments started to crumble. What must it have been like for her to spend her young life dealing with so much? Of course she was in no position to raise a child. She was in an impossible situation and had no one to help her. Her solution was easy, immediate, and free. Having the baby was the last thing she needed. I began to think of her as a victim who acted resourcefully in a desperate situation. Faced with real adversity and a lot less going for her, she was probably coping better than I was.

And then, looking in the mirror brushing my teeth before bed, I was hit by the biggest mindfuck of all: Maybe it never really happened; maybe it was another fake claim, like the sexual harassment complaint and the learning disability, made up to get attention. I was angry all over again. In a jag of self-pity, I longed for my earlier life, where it was so much easier to understand, to feel, and to think about everything.

The following week as I circulated around my classroom, I saw Valentina writing on the cover of a folder in thick blue marker. Well programmed to stay out of her orbit, I waited for her to walk across the room and sharpen her pencil and then drew close enough to read what she had written. It was an affirmation as intriguing and opaque as she was: "Haters can go kill theyselves. I'm in my rocket ship and I ain't coming down."

As always, her words were original, surprising, and spot-on. I paused, leaned against my bookshelf, and for a quick instant borrowed her vivid escape fantasy. I pictured myself in a silver spaceship orbiting the earth, alone, silent, and at peace. Since I couldn't thank her for that gift, I just thought, *Amen, sister, amen.*

CHAPTER 10

Old School

THE SCHOOL YEAR was wearing hard on the faculty and kids alike, and spring break in April couldn't come any sooner.

My family had adamantly requested our presence at Easter dinner in my hometown of Rochester, New York. An atheist Jew and a lapsed Catholic, Sam and I were normally a hard sell for the holiday, but the invitation was multipronged and forceful. First, my mother lobbed a call into our answering machine with a throaty chorus of "In your Easter bonnet, with all the frills upon it."

My sister Lynn, who still lived in Rochester, followed it up with a bald: "You better get up here while there is still a city to visit."

It was true, Rochester was a city in distress. The neighborhood where I grew up, adjacent to a now-closed Xerox factory, was once a safe and stable working-class enclave. Now it was fast descending into a Rust Belt dystopia. My parents had their car stolen several times, gang activity was rampant, and the childhood home of my best friend growing up was now a crack den. In 1982, my family was scared about my going to Fordham University in the Bronx; now, twenty-five years later, I was afraid for them.

Sam and I conceded and made the weekend trip, which we could barely afford. After the Easter feast, we all sat in my parents' elegant crimson living room, surrounded by my mother's treasures, half of them seemingly from churches, the other half from bordellos: candelabras, incense burners, an oversize Buddha she had adorned with an Easter bonnet, a pair of gilded Spanish crucifixes, and a tiny Japanese netsuke of a woman playing with herself in a bathtub. As children, our friends were bewildered or intrigued (and we, in turn, embarrassed or proud) by the mad, eclectic thrift-store montage. In their living rooms, by contrast, Ethan Allen ruled the roost.

The conversation eventually turned to my unhappy new profession. Nora was sympathetic: "I know it's been brutal for you. The first year is bad for just about everybody, but you seem to have landed in a really tough spot."

"But you're in the home stretch now. The end of the year will be here in no time," Lynn said. She, too, knew what I was up against, having spent time as a counselor in a very tough public middle school before becoming a therapist to the underserved.

My mother added, "They sound like a bunch of little creeps to me. Where are their parents in all this? Remind me, why are you doing this again?"

My father gave her the stink-eye, fearing more talk of teachers as losers. Then he added his two cents: "Kids have no respect these days, no regard for authority. Imagine if you ever said those things to your teachers at St. Anselm's. Those priests were great role models and teachers, and you showed them the respect they deserved."

The beat-down teacher in me wanted to buy my father's version of the good ol' days, but being back home and just down the block from my old high school had me thinking back to my own ninth-grade year. "Come on, Dad, some of them were hardly role models, and they sure weren't all good teachers. Think about Father Tenner—and he was the goddamn *principal*."

As I cleared the table, my sisters laughed at the mention of his name and infamous story. While loading the dishwasher, I paused to look out the kitchen window into the darkness. I was taken back to 1978, and the opening-day Mass of my Catholic high school, St. Anselm's.

"Men, honor needs to be restored to this school. I have been brought back to St. Anselm's all the way from Texas to lead it on the path to honor, to take it back from softness, from weakness. Remember, every action you take is a reflection on you, your school, and your church. We are all soldiers in Christ," Father Tenner boomed.

If there were a giant American flag behind him, you could be forgiven for thinking he was General Patton. He was well over six feet tall, barrel-chested, with a shock of white hair. Depending on the topic of conversation and his blood-alcohol level, his face alternated between sheet-white and beet-red.

"Men, let us now bow our heads and pray to almighty God." He looked toward the ceiling briefly and then let his head fall loose to his chest. The heads of six hundred pimply, awkward, and over-gelled boys dutifully dropped in unison and droned out some prayer. Even though it was my first day of high school, I had already figured out that when Father Tenner said pray, you damn well had better pray.

During my nine years in a coed grammar school, the nuns like dear Sister Concepta had fattened us on charity, grace, and kumbaya, and I was the most gorged goose of all. This kind of macho religiosity from Father Tenner was bewildering. Jesus was a he-man? Since when?

As I was scurrying out of school later that day, Father Tenner cornered me.

"Boland, right?"

"Yes, Father."

"Dave Boland, class of fifty-three, is that your father?"

"Yes."

"Dave Boland, who intercepted that pass against Boys Town and put this school's football team on the map?"

"I guess."

"You guess? Your father was a great athlete and brought honor to this school. From the looks of you, I am not sure we can expect the same," he said, scanning my ninety-pound frame.

"No, Father, I don't play football, if that is what you're asking." He dismissed me with a toss of his head.

The next day, I was horrified to walk into my algebra class and see Father Tenner scribbling with a pencil at the lectern. It was bad enough being under the same roof as the man, but now he was going to try to teach me math, my lifelong weakness? "Oh well, it's Bum, Bum, Boland!" he shouted.

It was worse than my worst nightmare. He was like no other teacher I'd ever had. He would bellow and charge and flip over the desks of the defiant and the stupid. He punched, shoved, and screamed while ranting about coefficients and polynomials. Like some scheme from the Cultural Revolution, we were assigned seats according to our GPAs. For almost the entire year, I was in the last row near the side blackboard. I wouldn't have been surprised if he'd arrived with dunce caps for us.

Word problems, normally the only kind of problem I could solve, were converted into baffling sports analogies. He would say, "If tailback Joe is running a safety at 15 miles per hour and Tom is running toward the end zone at 18 miles an hour, who will arrive first?" or "Not isolating the variable is like not isolating the opponent's best wide receiver."

Father Tenner's favorite trick was to pretend to give you a congratulatory handshake for answering a question. If the answer was wrong, he turned his extended hand into a fist and punched you fast in the chest. I am not sure which was worse, the violence or the psychological warfare of thinking you actually got something right. Math through terror, however, seemed popular with almost every other student. Thirty boys, blissing on your misery, cheered him on as you sat there smarting. They lapped it up, and I sat there in blank horror. Parents praised the priest "who knew how to deal with boys."

Father Tenner's plan to revitalize the school was taken from the *Triumph of the Will* playbook. Naturally, degenerate artists and intellectuals were relegated to the margins. On the same night our drama club made do with a potluck of our mothers' casseroles onstage, the football team was treated to a sit-down steak banquet for its routing of our upscale rival, McQueen Jesuit. There were other rallies, parades, and award ceremonies where strapping lads were praised for their gridiron prowess.

In public and private, I loathed Father Tenner, yet when you least expected it, he would pull you aside and say something funny or even a bit kind. "I know you're terrible at math, Bum Bum Boland, but at least I see you're trying. People stupider than you have done this."

After a ten-month blur of failed quizzes, Ds, and probationary notices, the year came to a close. I took the state algebra exam and waited for what I was sure would be a notice of summer school.

A week after school ended, on the first warm night of summer, my father and I sat on the couch watching the eleven o'clock news. The perky announcer glanced up and said the kind of thing most students only dream of hearing about their school: "Shame struck St. Anselm's Academy tonight."

My father stared straight ahead, desperate not to make eye contact with me. And then the tape rolled. In all its choppy and hazy glory, it showed the school's maroon-and-white station wagon. It slowly pulled up to a buxom woman in purple hot pants and a halter top. She leaned into the car.

The voice-over gravely announced, "Principal John Tenner of the St. Anselm's Academy was arrested last evening for soliciting a police decoy posing as a prostitute." I felt my cheeks get warm.

The camera focused on his face. He leaned out the window and slurred, "Hey, baby. I've got twenty bucks, can you..." *BLEEP BLEEP BLEEP* went the TV. The last frames showed two officers leading Father Tenner, handcuffed, hunched over at the waist and trying to cover his beet-red face, into a paddy wagon. He was never to be heard from again. The whole thing felt so surreal and, at the same time, ominous. Had that really just happened?

My grades arrived by mail the next day; I dodged the summer school bullet with a whopping 67 on the state exam.

I snapped out of my reverie and rejoined my family's conversation about old-school Catholic education.

Sam, who had been educated by hippies at a crunchy private school on a former farm in Oregon, was horrified by what he heard. "I don't get it. How can anyone learn under those conditions?"

Lynn said, "Well, Eddie, to your credit, you are creating a classroom that is the opposite of Father Tenner's. You are trying to be really inclusive and caring."

I agreed, but the more I thought about it, I also had to acknowledge an uncomfortable truth. "You know, guys, I don't like to admit this, but truth be told, way more learning happened in Tenner's class than is happening in mine today. For the most part, the man did get results. Most of the guys loved him."

"But at what cost?" said Lynn.

"I won't teach by fear, the way he did. I couldn't if I wanted to."

Sam added, "But it's not just one or the other. There has to be some kind of middle ground between mob rule and that junta at St. Anselm's."

"If only I could strike that balance. I'm just not sure where to find it," I said.

Nora had the last word: "I've been teaching for a long time now, and my only answer is that there are no easy answers. I wish I had more for you, but I really don't."

Sam and I filed up to bed and set the alarm for an early flight back to New York. Fortified with a weekend of family love and lessons from the past, I steeled myself for the return to Union Street.

CHAPTER 11

Lil' Mickey, a Disciple of Soul

SMACK! POP! WHACK! POW!

The sounds were right out of a brawl on a Saturday-morning cartoon, but this was all too live, all too real. In this uneven matchup, Dannisha easily had a hundred pounds and four inches on her opponent, Lil' Mickey. She landed her punches well, jabbing with her left, slapping with her right. His face rippled like jelly, and the crowd of fellow ninth graders went wild. In a final coup de grâce, Dannisha reached behind her without looking, grabbed a small cardboard box of largely untouched art supplies, and started to pummel Lil' Mickey on the head with it. With every swing, colored paper and markers flew out of the box like a burst piñata.

Mickey Vega had been a terror from the minute he set foot in school. Skinny and skittish, he was incapable of sitting still or staying quiet. He had light copper skin and a left eye that wandered furiously. He roamed the halls at will, boldly sporting everything contraband—an iPod, Cheez-Its, a chunky outdated cell phone, a Yankees cap, and the gang colors of the Bloods. Despite looking and acting just like Kameron and the other bad boys, Mickey didn't enjoy the same popularity. His classmates couldn't stand him. Even they sensed that his antics weren't just fun and games, but that something inside his brain was truly haywire.

Mickey harassed a different girl every day of the week, but on that fateful afternoon, he'd chosen to bother the heretofore silent and supersized Dannisha with one of his favorite routines. In true "gangsta" style, his baggy jeans seemed to float magically somewhere between his rear end and his knees, with his Old Navy boxers in full view. While she was trying to read, he slid his skinny behind down her desktop and got his crack too near her face. He had pulled this trick before with some pretty tough girls, and it was usually met with mere annoyance. They'd swat him away like a fly. No one would have suspected that Dannisha would be the one to put him in his place. But without a word, she picked him up by his scrawny waist and immediately sent him to the floor like a toy a child had grown tired of. *Bam!*

I had not been involved in any kind of fight since the sixth grade, when I unsuccessfully took on a local bully over a perceived school-yard insult. Thirty-five years later, I was both rusty and terrified, but also convinced that Dannisha could actually kill Mickey in my classroom right in front of my eyes. For an instant, I wondered what clever headlines the *New York Post* would create for such a story.

Before the school year started, the new faculty members had been read the riot act by Seth, a math teacher and our union representative: "Whatever you do, don't get in the middle of a fight. If you get hurt, you are not covered at all by health insurance or disability. It's not worth the risk. Just call Security."

It sounded so logical at the time, but school security was a distant hope at the moment. We were on the third floor, and no matter of emergency ever brought the guards up three flights. The first time I'd called down to have a student removed, the class laughed as I held the handset in my sweaty palm listening to it ring for a full minute, and a voice taunted me from the back of the room: "You crazy? They ain't draggin' their black asses up here. Think they got room service here, mister?"

I swallowed hard and stepped into the fray, squeezing myself into the flurry of flying limbs. As I tried to push them apart, Dannisha, clawing indiscriminately, scratched my neck bloody and hit me with the box of art supplies. Just when I thought the classroom couldn't get any louder, my entry into battle inspired even more deafening screams and cheers from the onlookers.

Yerfrey, a sweet kid who had recently arrived from the Dominican Republic, was the only other person in the room who seemed to recognize that something dangerous was happening. Wide-eyed and flustered, he went scurrying into the hallway to get help, pushing through a growing group of kids standing in the doorway, watching the show.

Of all people, it had to be Seth who marched in to see me ignoring his advice and disobeying union rules. With great difficulty, he pulled Dannisha off Mickey and muscled her out of the classroom. Dannisha was bellowing at the top of her lungs and nursing a bloody eye. Seth pulled her down the hallway, where she collapsed in a bawling heap. Brad, the English teacher from two doors down, then removed a dazed and unusually quiet Mickey. Just when everyone thought the fracas was over, Dannisha broke free from Seth and went charging down the hall for another round with Mickey. Luckily, Brad stopped her in her tracks.

Drawing on the surge of adrenaline that was coursing through my veins, I pulled myself together and, without a word about what had just happened, started teaching again, returning to our lesson on the role of the United Nations in global conflicts. I dragged a broken-down VCR in front of the kids and showed a clip from *Hotel Rwanda* to illustrate the challenges faced by UN peace-keepers. As they half watched, I stood in the back of the room discreetly blotting the blood from my neck.

At the very end of class, I summarized the lesson in a robotic voice: "So, as you saw in the clip, a UN peacekeeper comes from a different country outside of the conflict; he's lightly armed and avoids direct engagement where possible. He enters the battle only as a last resort."

Fat Clovis, now the unquestioned leader of the class's Greek chorus, smiled broadly and guffawed. "Just like you, mister. Just like you."

Mickey's offenses continued to pile up, even after the fight with Dannisha. In complete frustration, I had summoned his grandmother from the rough-and-tumble streets of Bed-Stuy for an intervention of sorts with the principal, the social worker, his Special Education teacher, and me.

Three days later Granny Wardwell arrived, unsteady on two clattering canes, at the first-floor nurse's office, which we had commandeered because she couldn't climb the stairs to my room. She had put on her Sunday best for the occasion, including a pink, somewhat misshapen, church-lady hat that had seen many an Easter. A hulking far older brother accompanied her on the trip. He didn't speak, wouldn't shake hands, and turned his chair away from us with disdain. We were packed in the tiny space, practically knee to knee.

Before we even sat down, she announced she had used her last dime getting a car service to the school. Everyone shifted uncomfortably at that news. As if from the pulpit, she pointed to Mickey and preached, "This is a good boy, a sweet boy, a boy who has a shelf full of awards and trophies at home, a child who loves history. I am shocked to hear him described as disruptive."

Everyone looked at me, and I looked at Mickey.

He sat there oblivious, humming and pretending not to listen as I recited his rap sheet: the now-famous incident with Dannisha, a food fight with Eugenio laced with Mexican slurs, the gum-in-the-Koran episode, and the vandalization of the computer room in full view of the catatonic substitute teacher whom he kept calling Mrs. Doubtfire. (His assessment was unfortunately on the mark; the resemblance was uncanny.)

"Oh, we have never had this kind of situation before," Mrs. Wardwell protested. "We may be poor, but I raised this child right and in the eyes of God. He has the blood of all people in him, black, Spanish, white, even American Indian. How can he be prejudiced?"

There was more uncomfortable shifting and silence from my colleagues. Suddenly sensing that I had misplayed my hand, I let my eyes float between cheery health posters touting the joys of flossing and frequent hand washing as I thought of a response.

"Well, I don't think behavior like this just starts overnight—" I was interrupted by a sudden, ferocious snore from the brother, his back still to us. As he exhaled, his bristly neck roll shook violently. Grandma poked him in the ribs to stop the distraction.

She ignored me and looked directly at Mei. "I don't know how long Mr. Boland has been teaching, but maybe he isn't experienced enough yet to understand kids like Mickey." What made it worse was that she said this with Christian compassion instead of anger. My face reddened and my hands went cold.

I started to speak again, but she interrupted me. "As I understand it, Mickey has been repeatedly provoked by his classmates. He commutes over an hour to come here and there is no one else from our neighborhood here. He's new and doesn't know many other students."

Challenging anyone's beaten-down grandma is difficult. Taking on one with dentures so rickety that she had to hold them up with her thumb is impossible. She had me on the ropes.

"I am not feeling well and need to get home," said Grandma. She poked the sleeping giant again. "Let's go, RJ."

I shook her hand, but she wouldn't look at me. Disapproval from a sweet old lady hit me hard. Maybe it was true that my lack of experience brought out the worst in Mickey. Maybe he *was* as much victim as perpetrator.

"Well, we'll continue to monitor the situation here and keep you informed of his progress. Every student can and will continue to be successful here," said Mei with a bright smile. I could tell she couldn't wait for the whole thing to be over.

A week later, Katy, Mickey's Special Ed teacher, received his primary school Special Education file and left it in my mailbox. It was packed with offenses going back to the second grade: incident reports, an expert diagnosis classifying him as "antisocial," and a bunch of faded Polaroids of a cheery classroom that looked like the Manson family had paid a visit—an overturned bookshelf, shredded artwork, and a chair in pieces.

I shut the file. I had been played by a church lady.

Months passed and Mickey's crimes continued unchecked. I had devoted a large part of the spring to a world religions unit. In an effort to undo some of the prejudices of my young charges, I threw myself into the lessons. To make it all seem relevant, I planned a field trip as the culmination of the unit, where we would visit a Jewish synagogue, a mosque, and a Buddhist temple. I was especially worried about bringing Mickey on this trip. He often made anti-Semitic comments, and a week before, he'd desecrated a picture of a prostrate Muslim praying toward Mecca by turning it into an anal sex scene. So naturally, of the fifty permission slips I received back, the first was from Mickey's grandmother, signed in her shaky hand. I let out a little whimper.

On a gorgeous May morning, a group of about fifty kids and four teachers set out for the Ninety-Seventh Street mosque. I had spent a lot of time teaching my kids about mosque etiquette: removing their shoes, washing their hands, and, for the girls, donning head scarves. For many, it took some convincing that these courtesies wouldn't violate their Christian faith and "make them" Muslims. It didn't help matters when Kendra, up until then a devout Christian, showed up at school the morning of the trip wearing a long hijab and announced she was becoming a Muslim. This scene sent the kids atwitter, saying that Mr. Boland was hell-bent on converting everyone to Islam.

When we arrived, the kids were impressed by the mosque and its stately minarets, which took up a whole city block. The kindly imam droned through an unsolicited forty-minute sermon, delivered through half-closed eyes. His accent was so thick, he could have been reciting a Chuck E. Cheese's menu for all we knew, but whatever he said, he quickly used up our already scarce supply of "Please be on your best behavior in public." To my surprise, Mickey didn't act worse than anyone else. As we exited, Jahmellah, one of the Muslim students, gave a touching lecture to a group of girls about how central chastity was to her faith and that her mother made her go to a "special doctor" to ensure that her virginity was still intact. (The week before, I had intercepted a note being passed back and forth between her and a group of boys that included "Do you want to give us all hand jobs?" But the word *hand* was scratched out and they had upped the ante to blow jobs. From her scribbled responses, it seemed as if the requests were under active consideration.)

On the subway to our next destination, as the students were screaming and slapping one another, I wondered who they misunderstood more, the Jews or the Muslims. September 11 hadn't helped the image of the Muslims for this group; many of my students lived in downtown Manhattan, and much of their youth had been defined by the event. But there were plenty of instances when I'd heard the phrase "rich fuckin' Jews" in the hallways as well, often within earshot of Jewish teachers struggling to make car payments or cover their kids' orthodontist bills. As awful as it was, the anti-Semitism never really got addressed. There were simply too many other fires to put out.

We arrived late and rowdy at Temple Emmanu-El, a chunk of formidable limestone on Fifth Avenue, the toniest temple in New York. At the visitors' center, I checked in with a portly Latino security guard. He craned his neck over the desk to see where all the noise was coming from and rolled his eyes when he saw my crew terrorizing a hot-dog vendor outside.

He flipped through a stack of papers attached to a clipboard without looking up. "You're Union Street? You're really late, y'know that? Tell those kids to be quiet and wait outside till you are escorted in by your guide."

A few minutes later, out tottered Hadassah. Hunched but perky, she was probably kissing eighty and was five foot two at most, even with the assistance of a smart pair of cork wedges. She looked up at me through oversize Philip Johnson–like glasses and asked me a few perfunctory questions as the screams, shouts, and profanities reached a crescendo outside. I pulled her out of sight of my students and spoke frantically, sputtering, "Sometimes they get so out of hand, but…they really don't mean what they say half the time, and…we tried to study Judaism, but…and there is this one boy, Mickey."

She fixed me with a stare, part Golda Meir, part Dr. Ruth. "Don't you worry about a thing, my dear. Oh, they'll listen to *me*," she declared. We entered the massive sanctuary. The kids were immediately awestruck. Many of them were used to storefront evangelical operations and the low-rent kingdom halls of the Jehovah's Witnesses. Sunlight poured in through stories-high stained-glass windows. Soaring organ music swelled in the vast space. They filed into the pews quietly. I was relieved to see Mickey sit in a row at the back by himself.

Hadassah mounted the altar, and with one smooth gesture pulled a high-tech wireless headset down from over her ear to her mouth. Janet Jackson had nothing on her.

"That's it, Sebastian, thank you," she said into her headset. The blasting organ went silent midnote. It was clear who ran the show here. She then held forth for a half hour about her faith, its history, and the temple. And by God, as she'd promised, they listened to her. I should have been delighted at their behavior, but instead I sank into a shame spiral about my shortcomings as a teacher. *What has she got that I ain't got? Are they cutting her slack because she's old? Female? Short? Maternal? The last time I tried to lecture for even five minutes, there was immediate unrest. Now here they are, listening raptly like members of the Temple Sisterhood. What gives?*

"Questions?" Hadassah said finally. My abdomen tightened.

Figgy threw up his hand. "How much does it cost you to heat this place every month?"

"Well, no one has ever asked me that before. I don't know." She sounded perplexed. "Probably a lot." It may have seemed bizarre or cheeky to her, but it was a logical question for a kid whose mother was struggling to pay the rent for a basement apartment in the Bronx.

"How do you change a lightbulb up in here?" Fat Clovis called out as he craned his neck up to the ornate ceiling.

She just chuckled.

"Are you Jewish?" asked Warren.

"What a silly question! Of course I'm Jewish."

"Well, that security guard back there, he works here and he don't look too Jewish to me," he shot back. *Touché.*

"Good point," she conceded.

"Why do the Jews love black and white so much?" asked Kate.

"Oh, you mean the cookie. Yes, I love black-and-white cookies. They're great with coffee."

"The Jews invented Oreos?" Kate asked.

Hadassah looked even more puzzled.

"Jews make Oreos? No wonder they're so rich," someone mumbled. My eyes immediately darted back to Mickey, but I was relieved to see him blankly staring into space.

I tried to come to Hadassah's rescue. "I think Kate means in their choice of clothing." Kate nodded yes.

Hadassah again seemed mystified, and with a sweep of her hand she alluded to her colorful floral-print dress with pride.

I intervened again. "Many of our students come from the Lower East Side. I think she means the Hasidic community."

"Oh, *them!*" She seemed eager to distance herself. "That's a good question. They like things very old-fashioned."

Wilson Chan, a perennial wiseass who specialized in making adults uncomfortable, took his shot. "Do you hate Muslims?"

She gasped. "Why, no! I don't hate anybody and..." Before she could finish, she was drowned out by Mickey's raspy voice screaming from the last row. I cringed. I knew this was coming.

"You dumb bitches, don't you listen to nothin' Mr. Boland tells you in class? The Jews and the Muslims are related through daddy Abraham. It's family fuckin' feud over there, and it has been for a long time. What's the matter with you? You don't listen."

The sacred setting was perfect for an emotional thunderclap. I was literally speechless. Mickey, of all people, had listened to something in class and really got it. Mickey—asleep. Mickey—with the headphones always on. Mickey—with his head forever out the window. How in God's name did that sink in? How did *anything* sink in? *Mr. Boland?* I was shocked that he even knew my name after ten months. What the hell else did he manage to learn? My mind raced. Maybe they were all getting it, learning on the sly, and faking stupidity just to torture me. Just "frontin'." Maybe there was hope after all.

As I was leaping from idea to hopeful idea about the power of teaching, I suddenly realized that all eyes, including Hadassah's, were on me, waiting for me to light into Mickey for his irreverence and profanity. Hadassah was miffed. I heard myself giving a perfunctory reprimand, but I was still enjoying the afterglow of my tiny victory. In a biblical echo, "the least of my brethren" had learned something from me. I felt giddy, dizzy, and drunk, all at the same time.

As we filed back out of the sanctuary and onto the street, a passage from *A Streetcar Named Desire* flashed into my head. Blanche Dubois was right: "Sometimes—there's God—so quickly!"

The final leg of our trip was to a large Buddhist temple in Chinatown, housed in a former pornographic movie theater not far from the school. I was coming down from the adrenaline rush of Mickey's revelation and barely had the energy to keep the kids in line. In front of a large gilded statue of Buddha, a subdued Buddhist nun in gray robes with a heavy accent and a mouthful of braces gave us a blessedly brief overview of twenty-five hundred years of Buddhism. At this point, even I was having a hard time paying attention. She closed our visit by inviting me to choose a student to ring the temple bell, an enormous bronze thing imported from China and hanging from a tall, elaborately engraved wooden tripod.

I foolishly offered Marius Owens as a volunteer. He grabbed the ringer, a wooden log hanging on chains, and ran with it like a maniac full force into the bell. A deafening peal rang out. I was certain he had cracked it. The nun covered her mouth in horror and quickly went over to inspect the bell. Other nuns and concerned worshippers came out of nowhere. To my relief, it was undamaged. Before I could say anything to Marius, his classmates let him know he had crossed the line: "Chill the fuck out! Why you wiling, man? It's religious in here!" I was glad they took over because I didn't have the reserves for one more chewing-out that day.

Even the nun had lost her Zen cool. "What is the *matter* with these children? You should not bring them back here," she said as she rushed us toward the exit. After a final profuse apology from me and a forced one from Marius, we filed out of the candlelit temple and into the brilliant sunshine to walk back to school. I was spent.

Maybe it was the warm spring air or being liberated from the school building, but romance and vulgarity were in the air. Several established couples, led by Nestor and Blanca, joined hands as we made our way back to school. Singles were flirting up a storm with off-color jokes and frisky horseplay. To my surprise, attention suddenly turned my way.

"Hey Mr. Boland, you got a girlfriend?"

"No," I answered, for what was probably the two hundredth time that year.

From the beginning, I had always vowed that if asked, I would never lie about my sexuality, but I hadn't been directly asked. For whatever reason, though, that afternoon Stephan Epperson broke through and said what no one else had the temerity to ask all year: "Have you got a boyfriend?"

Without much thought, I answered with a simple "Yes."

I realized what I had said as it was leaving my mouth. In my fog, I lacked the energy or even the will to brace myself. I had already been shredded and fed to the crowd; there was little left to devour. I looked into the sun and numbly waited for the onslaught. I heard a short giggle, a tiny gasp, mostly silence.

"Have you got a picture?" Blanca asked with genuine curiosity.

Warily, I pulled out my phone, which had a tiny magenta sticker-photo of Sam on the back, smaller than a postage stamp. They gathered around the phone and inspected the image with care and intensity, as if they had uncovered a rare coin.

"Ohh, Mr. Boland's boyfriend is *black!*" Stephan said.

"No, he's not, actually," I said.

"Ohh, Mr. Boland's boyfriend is *Lat-in!*" said Nestor.

"No, he's actually Jewish."

"Ohh, Mr. Boland's boyfriend is *rich*," a voice at the back said.

"No, he actually makes very little money."

"Jewish? Oh yeah, that's right, I heard when you can't tell what they are, they Jewish."

"Does he got a big dick?" asked Fat Clovis in an earnest tone, as if he were asking Sam's name.

I conjured a last vestige of professionalism and tried to act indignant. "That's really inappropriate, Clovis. What are you thinking, even asking about that?"

"Yeah, tell us about that *salchicha!*" said someone at the back of the pack.

"*Salchicha! Salchicha! Salchicha!*" they chanted in unison. The Chinese mothers and Hasidic men from the neighborhood gave us a wide berth and shot disapproving looks. The chorus grew louder and more raucous, but it wasn't the hateful chants of *The Lord of the Flies*. It was jolly and real and human. And they seemed happy for me. Where was all that hate? Why hadn't I just done this from the start? I blushed.

I was standing on East Broadway surrounded by a group of thuggy teenagers chanting about my boyfriend's junk. This was to be the greatest moment of communion with my students?

I took what I could get. Victory, thy name is *salchicha*.

CHAPTER 12

The Ivy Curtain

"THIS PLACE IS sweet. Dope as fuck." Solomon Figueroa pulled off his knockoff Sean John sunglasses and squinted into the white winter sun on Columbia University's campus. He was jaunty, light-skinned, and round-faced. "A man could get used to this kinda school."

He gazed up at the statue of *Alma Mater*. "Who's she?" he asked, a little out of breath from having sprinted up the stairs. As she had for more than one hundred years, Columbia's famous icon, personified as Athena, sat in glazed majesty, overlooking the imposing campus. Draped, busty, and bronze, her upheld arms formed a commanding *W*. The Quad was quiet and lightly dusted with snow, and only a hint of ambient city noise wafted in. Even though Solomon and a few of his classmates lived nearby in Harlem, no more than a subway stop or two away, none of them had ever been to the storied campus. They were suitably awed.

I was pleased by his curiosity and was ready to remind him about our unit on Greek mythology or tell him how the Weathermen had planned to blow the statue up in the sixties. But before I could say a word, he and the group of ten other boys were already on to the next thing—the quicksilver nature of the teenage mind.

It was early February and we had just arrived on campus for

a Model UN competition. Since Union Street had a focus on international studies, Model UN was supposed to be an integrated part of the curriculum and a prominent extracurricular activity. I was serving as the coach and chaperone for the ninth-grade boys' team. Secretly, I hated it. I was forty-five and had a master's degree, but I could barely understand the club's bureaucratic rigmarole. So how was I supposed to explain it to the kids? How does a delegate from Vanuatu introduce an unmoderated caucus on potable water desalinization? Got me. *Robert's Rules of Order* seemed riveting in contrast. The kids didn't love it much either, though we were all pretty happy to get out of the classroom for a day.

A leggy blond undergrad bundled up in a Marmot bubble coat and carrying a backpack clacking with activist buttons strolled by. Solomon puffed up his chest, craned his neck, and gave her an overeager smile. Obliviously insulated by earbuds, she smiled back and nodded, wondering if she was supposed to know him. He put on his "Hey, ain't I handsome?" face and smoothed his cropped black hair.

"See that? Bitches can't get enough of my shit here."

"Solomon, check your language!" I said. At this point in the year, I had given up on any kind of profanity check, save the most egregious, because otherwise, language policing would have been my full-time job. But in public, I tried to keep up at least the illusion of propriety. He raised his palm to me to show he knew he was in the wrong.

To teachers and classmates alike, Solomon was easy to love and easy to hate: half smart-ass, half bighearted goofball. Our shared ambivalence grew out of the fact that he couldn't make up his mind about what kind of kid he wanted to be. Although I struggled not to think in such absolutes, I found that by high school most kids had decided which road they were going down. Frankly, there were good kids and bad kids and not so many in-betweens, but Solomon was a clear and confounding exception. His great flaw was that he was a consummate pleaser. (It takes one to know one.) He wanted the affirmation of both the bad-boy posse and the full faculty. Sometimes he wanted that love from everyone in the same hour.

I met him the first day of our advisory group, when I was still in a state of shock from my showdown with Kameron. Solomon acted differently than most of the boys. He looked me in the eye, shook my hand, and said, "In kindergarten, my teacher told my mother, 'Little Solomon has the qualities of a lawyer.' That lady was right. I'm a gonna be a lawyer." It was an impressive first showing. Impressive, that is, until an hour later, when he twisted gum in some new kid's hair and a shoving match ensued.

Solomon would make insightful comments about world history while simultaneously soaking spitballs in his copious chipmunk cheeks. (Spitballs seemed so old-fashioned, right out of *Ozzie and Harriet*, even to me, but I suppose some modes of misbehavior are timeless.) One day, after I caught him red-handed, ready to hurl a thoroughly spit-soaked, Ping-Pong ball–size wad of paper, he yelled, "Get away from me, you fuckin' faggot!" While it was always stinging to hear those words screamed in my face, this time I also felt a horrible sense of betrayal because I liked and respected this kid and thought he felt the same way about me. I expected more and he knew better. An hour after his tirade, he stood in the doorway with a heartfelt apology letter (unmandated by any authority) and yet another handshake.

At the time of the Model UN conference, we had recently reached a low point in our relationship. Because Mei had a soft spot for him, Solomon had been rewarded with a part-time job as a gofer in the school's main office. One of his tasks was to assist the school's attendance coordinator, an older woman from nearby Chinatown,

Mrs. Tang. There was no gentler and kinder person in the school. Even the bad kids were nice to her.

About two months into his time on the job, a shaken Mrs. Tang reported to Mei that she'd found Solomon standing silently in the staff coat closet near her things. That alone was a huge violation. She looked at her purse, which had been rifled through. A twenty-dollar bill was missing from her billfold. I had learned from an earlier incident that an experienced thief knows not to take everything, but just enough that the owner might not miss it. As you would hope with an attendance coordinator, she knew what was where in her purse at any given time.

I attended the subsequent disciplinary committee meeting as his adviser. It was harrowing. Instead of the usual stone-faced defiance kids usually presented, Solomon was outright bawling within minutes. "I didn't do it. I wouldn't do that to Mrs. Tang. She's nice." He kept repeating, "I'm a good kid." Like some kind of mythical creature, every day he rose to face the primordial struggle between good and evil. It was no fun to watch. He was fired from his job and written up. The theft was the last straw for many of the teachers. I tried to forgive him, but the whole incident left a terrible taste in my mouth, mostly because I knew how much he liked Mrs. Tang.

I would soon learn that it bothered me more than I knew. Not long after his firing, I held our advisory period in the computer lab to do a career interest survey. Solomon exchanged words that quickly grew heated with Big Mac, a quiet, surly giant of a kid who started the year at six foot five and seemed to add an inch a month. Normally the best of friends, they were suddenly exchanging blows. Big Mac's fist was the size of a ham and even a first halfhearted blow sent Solomon reeling. Now having had the experience of a few fights under my belt, I knew I had to act fast, particularly with a lot of expensive computers around.

I got in between the boys and pushed them apart. Big Mac seemed more than happy to be stopped from beating up his friend, but Solomon kept provoking him. He shouted to all who would listen that I had ruined his chances to take down "that punk-ass Big Mac." Solomon rushed up on me so close I thought our noses would touch. "FUCK YOU!" he blasted in my face. Without a second's thought, I seethed back at him, "No, Solomon, FUCK *YOU*!" My words came with a spray of spittle. Wild-eyed, Solomon turned and stormed out of the room.

My face was fiery with embarrassment. I fully expected the other boys to go apeshit after the exchange, but they were entirely unfazed. I was ready to apologize to them or maybe ask them not to say anything to Mei. But before I could say a word, they were glued to their computers playing the video games I had forbidden them from using.

I sat down and tried to make sense of what had just happened. I easily conjured a dozen good reasons why I'd fired those words back at him, but I wasn't fooling myself. Not a single one of them came close to justifying my behavior. I was a teacher who had just screamed a profanity at a fourteen-year-old boy, fueled by a temper I was fast becoming familiar with. Solomon had acted low, and I was right down there with him. I was lucky that Mei and Gretchen never got wind of it.

Solomon was given to grand pronouncements, and that morning at Columbia he let out a doozy. "I'mma go to this college, live in that dorm, and gonna get with that girl," he said, pointing to the undergrad who was about to round the corner. All the boys chuckled.

I shepherded my team into a nearby auditorium for the opening ceremony of the "UN General Assembly." Once the tiresome pomp and circumstance was over and the boys were dispatched to their "committees," I had a free hour to myself. I sat in an oak-paneled dining hall, sipped coffee, and considered Solomon's three wishes. Despite the best efforts of everyone at Union Street, did he or anybody else there have a viable chance of attending a college even remotely like Columbia? I glanced at a cluster of animated undergrads at the next table. They were flirting and shooting the shit, but I knew soon enough they would dive headlong into the books beside them, Thucydides and Thoreau, and notebooks packed to the margins with math I couldn't begin to understand. In my backpack was a stack of work sheets my students had turned in about the life of the prophet Muhammad. I was pretty sure not one of them had a single complex sentence in it (save for those by Byron and Lucas); some were even presented as cartoons—a concession I'd made to get my most reluctant writers in the game. I let out a barely audible moan.

I thought back to my first jobs out of college, when I'd worked as an admissions officer. As an undergrad at Fordham, I had been a star student tour guide, persuading nervous suburban parents that the Bronx was no longer burning and that the Jesuits would give their children a rigorous and moral education. Immediately after graduation, I was hired full-time by the Admissions Office. Two years later, I was over the moon when I landed a job as assistant director at Yale.

Working as a gatekeeper there gave me lasting insight into the formation of the American elite. On my first day, I stood across from the white clapboard office in New Haven and patted my twenty-four-year-old self on the back for getting hired. The building was adjacent to a leafy town square that was home to three churches. It was so damn Yankee, it looked like the Pilgrims and the Indians should have been sharing a bowl of succotash on its lawn. The surrounding campus was a stunning Gothic redoubt circled by a ring of deep urban decay.

In my first few weeks, the dean of admissions, Chan Morris, an avuncular, soft-core preppy, and the rest of the staff warmly welcomed me. They were an accomplished, diverse, and dedicated bunch. I was assigned to a cozy white office on the top floor with a gabled window and a sagging green leather couch. The floor was so warped with age that from time to time, it would send me and my wheeled desk chair inadvertently careening to the middle of the room without notice.

I had barely settled into my new digs when my colleagues and I were sent to scour the country looking for the best and the brightest young minds. In the fall, I went everywhere, from Charleston, West Virginia, to Kokomo, Indiana, to Montreal, to the Upper East Side of Manhattan. I was welcomed with varying degrees of energy and enthusiasm. In Ohio, an eager headmaster at a second-tier boarding school took me to a nice lunch and toured me around the campus in his convertible with the top down. At a large public school outside Detroit, I sat outside the cafeteria at a sticky table chatting with a representative from a local cosmetology school. Largely ignored by the students, we passed the time talking about the challenges of having very fine hair.

After the recruitment season wrapped up, the admissions staff returned in the late fall to New Haven and started the early-decision process. We would spend hour after hour poring over huge stacks of applications and green-bar computer reports. We parsed transcripts and called guidance counselors with questions like "So far, there seem to be three students ranked number one in your school who have applied to Yale. How do you account for that?" As a first step, two staff members read each application and assigned it an overall ranking of one (TAKE THIS KID!) to four (NO WAY).

The applicants were an impressive lot. A girl wrote a brilliant feminist essay—worthy of *Harper's*, really—about gender and socialization, revealing that she was a phantom serial farter in public and yet no one ever suspected because of her gender. An aspiring art major sent in a dazzling, poster-size pen-and-ink drawing of himself suspended high over the campus on a pair of gymnastic rings, his body forming a perfect *Y* for Yale. A Vietnamese refugee wrote about finding solace in a school in Nebraska after a near-death experience as a "boat person" when she was six years old. They all waltzed into the freshman class.

I also learned quickly that being too clever or familiar could backfire. A self-saboteur from Chicago wrote her essay about her fear of going to the dentist—in backward letters, colored pen, and a spiral "Yellow Brick Road" pattern; not the kind of thing an admissions officer wants to tackle in a mirror at midnight. A few years before, an overeager Eagle Scout from Pennsylvania on the wait list had pitched a tent on the lawn of the Admissions Office to show how ardently he was interested in attending. I am sure he enjoyed Haverford. Having the president of Stanford write you a letter of recommendation to Yale might seem like a good idea, but it resulted in a note from the dean that said, "If he's so enamored of the kid, let Stanford use a spot on him." It was the kiss of death when the daughter of a prominent alum from Columbus, Ohio, "discovered" she was one-sixteenth American Indian and checked the box for Native American.

And then there were the athletes. After fierce pressure from the athletic department, I had to admit a highly sought-after French Canadian hockey recruit. He had crappy grades, dismal scores, and his essay consisted of one sentence scribbled hastily in pencil: "I want to bèe a great hockey player," with an accent aigu hanging over the first *e*. *Alors!* To add insult to injury, he decided to go to Boston University.

After the preliminary votes were cast, the Admissions Committee was convened. Composed of faculty members, deans, and the most senior admissions representatives, they served as judge, jury, and executioner for the nearly fourteen thousand applicants.

Because competition was fierce and time short, you had to make your notes about the kids you were advocating for pithy and almost Zagat-guide-esque:

"Another hothouse flower with a perfect GPA, pass!"

"Virtuoso bassoonist and published poet at seventeen, an Eli to the core."

"Milquetoast, yes, but brilliant milquetoast."

"AP English teacher (Yale Class of '79) says she is the most original thinker she ever taught, not just a 'rara avis' but 'rarisima avis.'"

Any member of the committee could challenge you to back up your recommendation on any candidate in your region. After you made your case and answered their questions, the committee of eight or so would decide a candidate's fate on a wacky voting machine, rumored to have been specially designed by some nerdy electrical engineering major. It had small electric consoles from which members would anonymously flip a switch to light up either a thumbs-up green light, thumbs-down red light, or wait-list white light. Any applicant with more than a total of two reject and/or wait-list votes was automatically denied.

Because we had to get through about three hundred applications in each two-hour committee session, we developed shortcuts. You could look down at the names of four or five kids from one school who were terribly smart but not exceptional and say, "Reject the entire high school"; sometimes you could go further and say, "Reject the page," and send twenty kids on a single page of computer paper packing; or, most famously, "Reject the state" when it came to sparsely populated places like North Dakota or Wyoming.

Despite appearances, deciding which 14 percent of the applicants would get the golden ticket was really tough work. Once the children of alumni, recruited athletes, underrepresented minorities or regions, and students interested in underenrolled majors were considered, there wasn't much room for your generic genius. (By today's standards, by the way, 14 percent doesn't seem so brutal. In 2014, Yale got nearly thirty-one thousand applicants and accepted a mere 6.3 percent of them.)

The great majority of students we admitted were truly brilliant and had busted their tails to get there. But the fingerprints of privilege were still present. You just had to look a little harder to see them and resolve not to let them unfairly influence you. It wasn't immediately obvious that kids from elite feeder schools had been coached for years on their interviews, essays, and every conceivable form of standardized testing. Many of their college counselors had worked in elite admissions offices; their tutors had PhDs. They knew prominent alums who would write recommendations on thick, creamy bond paper. The letters arrived daily from white-shoe law firms, governors' mansions, and—in yet another shock to my blue-collar brain—vacation homes with proper names on engraved stationery: "The Manse, Little Compton, Rhode Island" or "Coral House, Hamilton, Bermuda."

As I tried to sort out fair from foul, Suzie, a perennial champion of the underdog, gave me advice I will never forget: "It's very easy to throw the prize at the kids who finish the race first, but always look at the incline they faced. That will tell you much more."

Once the more clear-cut cases had been decided, things got fuzzy, political, and sometimes unfair. It wasn't news to me that the process wasn't entirely meritocratic. It wasn't news to me that people were willing to use any and every angle to game the process. But it was a revelation about exactly what forms those advantages would take and how they were displayed: sometimes furtively, sometimes brazenly. The story of two applicants that year showed the collision of the old guard and the new world.

One late fall afternoon, I walked into the Admissions Office reception area. A lot of parents looked up nervously from the glossy promotional brochures they were perusing.

"Parker Shipley?" I asked, looking down at his interview card: an Andover student with a strong GPA and an impressive battery of test scores. A kid with a floppy blond wave of hair half covering his "aw, shucks" expression stood up.

"Hi, I'm Mr. Boland. I see you're from Rochester. Me too."

"Cool," he said, affable and at ease.

His father loomed behind him. "Rochester, eh? Is your father a Xerox man?" he said too loudly. He had that particular kind of patrician accent that somehow transcends geography, a woolly vocal braid of Julia Child and William F. Buckley.

"As a matter of fact, he is," I said.

He thought he saw an opening and pumped my hand eagerly. "Preston Shipley. I went to Xerox right out of Princeton. Yes, I'm a Princeton man, but I hope you won't hold that against Parker here. What class were you at Yale?" On a good day, I suppose I could pass for old Yankee/Ivy stock instead of shanty Irish.

"I didn't go to Yale," I answered matter-of-factly.

"I've been with Xerox for almost twenty years and know everyone in the executive suite," Mr. Shipley continued. "What's your father's name?"

"My dad isn't in the executive suite." I smiled, trying to give him a clue.

"Well, God knows, we need those engineers. There's no copiers without them!" He guffawed.

"He's not an engineer either." He looked puzzled, even troubled.

The son got the picture well in advance of the father. So did everybody else in the waiting room, judging from their expressions. The kid shifted awkwardly from one penny loafer to the other.

"My dad does shift work in the roll coating factory."

"Roll coating?" Mr. Shipley said. "Well. Oh. I don't get over there much." He looked blank and a little afraid, as if a member of the Khmer Rouge were about to interrogate his offspring.

"Well, it's nice to meet a fellow Rochesterian," I said, shaking his hand again.

This guy bugged me. His son had strong grades from a great prep school, along with good teeth and manners to match. Short of a sudden heroin addiction or spate of criminal activity, the kid was destined to go to one of probably twelve preordained institutions. Wasn't that enough?

A week after my interview with Parker, I sat in an overstuffed wing chair in the august lounge of the Yale Club of New York. The school's motto, "Lux et Veritas," was stitched into the carpet, embossed on my iced tea coaster, and emblazoned on the jacket of the old waiter who had begrudgingly brought me the iced tea. I was waiting for Hal Buckley and Francis Alcock, the two Old Blues who headed the local volunteer alumni group that conducted the alumni interviews required of all applicants. I had been forewarned by the dean of admissions that the New York group was chafing at the recent difficulty many of the Manhattan prep schools had had in getting students accepted to Yale, many of them children of alumni. Most of the schools had been feeders to Yale for nearly a century; one even predated the university's founding in 1701 by seventy years.

I had talked to them by phone but had never met them in person. Retired Wall Streeters, they were both old, smart, white, and pedigreed. With matching sets of wiry gray eyebrows, they could have been twins. We exchanged some initial pleasantries, and then I braced myself for the onslaught. "We used to hold our receptions for admitted students here, but your Admissions Office says it's too stuffy and we'd scare off kids who aren't from typical Yale backgrounds. Have you ever heard such twaddle in your life?" said Hal, the crankier of the two.

I scanned the room—a gorgeous mausoleum, majestic but imposing as hell, filled with scores of mean-looking old men who appeared ready to lower their *Wall Street Journals* and scream, "Get off my lawn!" in raspy unison.

"Why, it's such a striking space. Who wouldn't like it here?" I was trying to get on their good side.

"I just hope we have a better record in getting some kids in, because last year was, quite frankly, a debacle. A travesty, really," said Hal.

"I assure you I'll do my best to advocate for New York," I said with conviction, at the same time trying to suppress the images in my head of Statler and Waldorf, the pair of grumpy-old-men Muppets in the balcony.

Francis, who was somewhat friendlier, added, "We have a great crop of kids from Manhattan this year. Let's see. We've already discussed that Westinghouse Science Competition finalist from Stuyvesant, the Latvian fencer from the Trinity School, and the daughter of the dean at Columbia Law School whose father is a close friend of the president of the university."

"Yes, I saw your write-ups on all of them in the office. Very thorough. Thank you."

Francis leaned in and peered at me over the tops of his tortoise-shell glasses. "Over the weekend, we interviewed an extraordinary young woman from Miss Bartlett's School. She has real Yale polish. Great intellectual curiosity."

I checked the rumblings of a groan in my throat.

He continued. "But she lives in the South Bronx. From a very poor Puerto Rican family. Raised by a single, unemployed mother with three other children. She would be the first in her family to college. Her name is"—here he slowed down as if he were ordering a difficult-to-pronounce dish in a foreign restaurant—"E-mman-u-el-a Gut-i-err-ez." It was sweet how respectful of her name he was trying to be.

"Really?" I perked up. I knew from my experience at Fordham how rare a profile like hers was.

"She's part of this Project Advance program. Do you know about it?"

I shook my head, a little embarrassed not to. I was supposed to be the New York expert.

"They're doing amazing work identifying promising minority students in New York in middle school. They find these kids in the outer boroughs and get them scholarships to the very best schools. Looks like we are going to have several applicants just like her this year, and that's just great."

I realized that I had judged these guys wrong. They weren't just trying to safeguard spots for the kids of their alumni buddies.

They ran through some more names, handed over a new stack of interview reports, and slapped me on the back as I got in the elevator. Francis smiled. "Good luck in committee, Ed. Keep your shirts starched and your powder dry."

"And get our kids in," I heard from Hal as the door clanked shut.

I returned to New Haven a few days later and pulled Emmanuela's application out of a teetering pile. Her grades were strong and her Latin teacher had written a glowing recommendation, but she wasn't at the very top of her class. She was a first-rate debater, though, and had founded the school's Afro-Latina Alliance. When I presented her in committee, there was a long debate about her merits and careful consideration of the dozen or so other applicants from her school, each of whom could likely excel at Yale.

In the end, Emmanuela was muscled out of the running by some superstars in her class and put on the wait list. The alums were furious. I got a testy voice mail from Hal the day after the decision letters went out. "For Pete's sake, your office is sending us mixed messages. You tell us to find gems like Emmanuela with atypical backgrounds, but then you don't accept them. What gives?"

Years later, I came across her name working at Project Advance and learned that Emmanuela graduated from Columbia, where she did impressive work organizing Harlem tenants against a local slumlord. After graduation, she wanted to improve the lot of low-wage earners like her mother, and she became a widely respected union organizer and leader for health-care workers. In 2013, she ran for lieutenant governor of New Jersey on the Democratic ticket. We had missed a true gem. (Of the Project Advance students I admitted that year to Yale, two became doctors and one a law professor; one of the doctors has enrolled her own children at Dalton, her alma mater.)

As the Model UN competition was wrapping up for the day, I scanned the auditorium for my students. Unpracticed and intimidated, our team had ended up toward the bottom of the heap, but it was still great exposure for the kids. I spied Solomon in the auditorium, surrounded by some Columbia and Barnard students who had organized the competition. They pretty much ignored the winning Catholic girls' school team in their plaid skirts, and the prep school teams were old news to them, but they couldn't get enough of Solomon. You'd think he was a visiting dignitary. His swagger and humor were alluring to them—particularly coming from an "inner-city" kid whom they might have been ready to pity at first. Ironically, Byron, who had the best chances of anyone to attend a school like Columbia, sat one row behind Solomon, largely ignored by them.

I gave Solomon the signal it was time to go. He bounded up to me with a smile.

"Hey, mister. Those college kids, Jasmine and Taylor, say I should go to the Admissions Office and talk to them about applying here. They say they have lots of scholarships. And they have a law school here, too. It's famous."

I inwardly cringed. I was sure they thought they were doing God's work in pumping him up on Columbia.

"It's a little early for that. You're only in ninth grade. And if you want to go to college, Sol, you have to start applying yourself. You need to start working harder, way harder."

"I work hard," he protested. The smile was gone. He was close to shouting.

How could I use this moment to rally him, I wondered, to encourage him but without giving him false hope?

"Right now, you don't work hard enough. You have to work like Byron, even harder than Byron."

"Man, why you such a hater? Teachers are supposed to tell you you can do anything," he said angrily. His mood could turn on a dime.

"Of course you can go to college. I just want you to be realistic. And you need to know what it really takes," I said.

"I'm not going to some crappy college. I wanna go here. It's Ivy League. The best." He threw his arms up for emphasis, uncannily mimicking the *Alma Mater*.

Even if he did suddenly find a great work ethic and started studying twelve hours a day, did he have the natural horsepower to keep up in an environment anything close to this? I didn't know. This kid didn't have the benefit of Project Advance like Emmanuela or the advantages of being a Brahmin like Parker.

Our little team started to walk toward the subway. Although it was only four o'clock, the sun had already ducked behind the tall campus buildings. An amber glow from the lights of Low Memorial Library lit the campus. The whole way, Solomon provided running commentary on every female he saw, as well as his distaste for the modern sculptures we walked by.

"You know, mister, at lunch here it's all the soda you can drink," he said. He knew he had lost his cool in the auditorium and was trying to smooth things over.

"Really," I replied absentmindedly as I scanned the Quad for students that resembled mine. There were plenty of minority students, but to a knowing eye, most had middle-class or international trappings: better electronics, more expensive outerwear, and baseball hats worn at a different angle.

"And you can go back for more food as many times as you want."

"I didn't know that." I looked back at the campus as we started to descend into the subway. It was late enough in the day that the kids could be dismissed directly without going back to school.

"Later, mister." Back to his sweet self, he gave me a fist bump and a smile. He started to bound down the stairs to the uptown train. I headed downtown.

I was always proud about knowing the inner workings of elite places like this. People were always curious about it at cocktail parties and dinners. And, this knowledge signaled to them that I had come far. But for once, I wished I didn't know as much as I did about this shitty, clubby world. Who goes to what school and why. I didn't like knowing that Solomon's fate was already pretty well sealed by his ethnic surname, his lousy zip code, and his mother's measly income.

"'Night, Solomon," I called after him.

CHAPTER 13

Massacre of the Innocents

ONE APRIL AFTERNOON, my second-period class solemnly clomped into my classroom. They had never before entered so quietly, which made me immediately realize something was up. Where was their usual "Let's get ready to rumble!" energy? Without my urging, they all started pulling out pens and paper and answering the question on the board.

"Is everything okay?" I asked. No response, only frantic whispering from a group of boys near the windows.

The mystery didn't last long. Mei and two school security guards were soon at the door. The guards almost never made their way to the third floor, so I knew some serious shit had gone down.

The usually chipper Mei asked in her most severe voice, "Mr. Boland, may I see you for a moment?" In a mildly controlled panic at the doorway, she laid out the situation: In the science class that this group had just been in, somebody had smuggled in a pellet gun and shot Celeste Vouden twice in the neck and head. I gasped audibly.

The thought that anyone would shoot anything at Celeste was inconceivable. She was the meekest, sweetest child in the entire grade; she spoke only in soft, nervous fragments. She had a terrible skin condition on her arms and neck that looked like she had been severely burned. As if that weren't enough, she was nearly bald, but inexplicably wore a thin white headband every day.

As Mei spoke, I looked over her shoulder and watched as two teachers escorted Celeste down the hall. Her shoulders twitched as she sobbed.

"She's not hurt physically, but of course she's really terribly shaken up," said Mei.

The guards started rifling through everyone's bags and searching every nook and cranny of the room.

"Got it!" one of them announced as he pulled out the pellet gun that had been stashed up inside the thin space between the radiator and its cover.

All the kids who were in the aisle near the radiator were pulled out for interrogation immediately. I soldiered on with the lesson, but the level of distraction made it pointless. In the following days, Mei and Gretchen interviewed almost every kid in the class.

News of the gun was reported to the higher-ups, and soon mobile metal detectors manned by a belligerent group of unknown security guards appeared without warning. Up to that point, the teachers didn't have the time or really the desire to enforce the hated rule against electronics unless kids used them in class. When I took the job at Union Street, I was happy it wasn't the kind of school that needed metal detectors like Eugene Debs. Well, so much for that. The kids were furious with the searches because their iPods and phones were confiscated and only their parents could retrieve them by appointment. Nearby bodegas started running checking services where kids could leave their contraband for a dollar a day.

Gossip and rumors churned wildly around the school until finally about a week later Mateo Jimenez, one of my advisees, was fingered by three witnesses as the shooter. A crude ballistics assessment based on his seat assignment confirmed it. He cracked easily and soon confessed, via a Spanish translator.

There was widespread consternation in the teachers' lounge. The chorus was insightful as usual:

"Mateo? Really? That kinda-doughy kid who can't speak any English?" said Marquis, the history teacher.

"For a lot of kids, the only thing worse than being bullied is being ignored. Clearly, he was seeking to make his mark in the only way he could," added Sita in predictable social-worker-ese.

"I wouldn't give that kid credit for knowing how to operate a pencil, much less a pellet gun," said Trey.

"Was he one of the kids they caught pissing on the rolls of toilet paper in the stalls in the boys' room?" asked Mark, the phys ed teacher.

It was true that he wasn't a likely suspect. I'd gotten to know him pretty well through our time in the advisory group. Because of a cluster of unhappy family events in the rural Dominican Republic involving death and divorce, he had recently emigrated to live with a step-somebody and lots of half siblings in the nearby Baruch housing projects. Mateo didn't know them very well. They had all been here for a long time and were fully assimilated. One of them, a younger half brother in the middle school whom I often called on to translate, mostly just seemed embarrassed to be related to this "fresh off the boat" relative. I really felt for Mateo.

On the social radar of his grade, he was virtually nonexistent. He was chubby, pockmarked, and his clothes gave him away as an immigrant. His face bore a look of perennial shock. His English was the worst of anyone in the entire grade. The first day of school I had to repress a mix of laughter, pity, and shock when he, a fifteen-year-old, asked, "I make a pee-pee now?"

In class, when my poor Spanish proved useless in helping him, I employed native speakers to try to help him translate lessons, but they soon grew frustrated, and he sat there clueless. Next, I gave him some picture books about ancient Egypt that were targeted for first and second graders, a Spanish–English dictionary, and a watered-down work sheet asking the most basic questions. I got nothing.

I finally put Manfred, a native Spanish speaker, on the case, relegating the two of them alone to the back of the room. Manfred was not only the third-smartest kid in the ninth grade, after Byron and Lucas, but eager to please because, as rumor had it, he had the meanest father of anybody and would do anything to avoid a call to home from a teacher.

But after two classes, Manfred gave up and delivered his unvarnished opinion: "That fat kid you want me to help, his problem isn't English. He's just stupid—in any language. Oh, and he's lazy." Manfred handed the work sheet on ancient Egypt back to me, on which Mateo had written one thing: "I no want thees bebe book." I didn't blame him. What fifteen-year-old wants to be seen carrying around a book for first graders where Pharaoh is portrayed as a Smurf? But what was the alternative?

Even Marie, the ESL teacher, didn't have much more insight than I did. "It happens a lot in the third-world countries without mandatory schooling. You get sixteen-year-olds from rural areas who have had little consistent education. Sometimes, they hardly know the alphabet. Who knows what that kid knows?"

Mateo was sentenced to the same suspension school in the Bronx as Kameron, but he would be exiled there for the entire remainder of the school year. On his last afternoon at Union Street, I unlocked the coat closet where my advisees kept their things. He seemed somewhere between stunned and oblivious as I helped him put his few possessions into a crinkled red plastic bag I'd found.

"Buena suerte. At your new school, *a tu nuevo escuela, sea bien,"* I stammered, continuing to mix and mangle the Spanish.

He looked at me and said matter-of-factly, "I'm not bad."

"I know that, Mateo, *es verdad, yo se eso."*

Although what he did was serious, I still had compassion for him. I, too, had entered a hostile new world and made some naive decisions, but I had immeasurably more to fall back on than he did. How could I judge him?

Mateo was soon gone, but questions remained. It didn't add up. He was too innocent to think it all up on his own. He was also remarkably impressionable. Somebody had put him up to it.

I scanned the faces of his classmates, the students in my second-period class. There was no shortage of possible culprits.

During a lunch period the following week, I came across two of my freshmen, Jaylisa and Philippa, hiding in a stairwell. They were taking turns applying an overpowering perfume that smelled like a freshly opened box of Fruity Pebbles. Students were forbidden from wandering the halls during lunch unless they had permission from a teacher to be upstairs for extra help. I was about to send them packing with my usual barking when I had an idea. After all, I wanted information, and I had two of the best gossips in the grade over a barrel. In small ways, I was starting to see the opportunities between all the rules.

"Ladies, you know you aren't supposed to be up here during lunch."

"We know," they said in sullen unison.

"But it's not a problem. Why don't you come to my room for lunch today?" I said. They looked at each other warily.

My bribery continued with a bag of off-brand barbecue potato chips that I'd bought at a nearby bodega. "So, I'm sure you've been interviewed by the principal like everybody else, but I know you two and I bet you know the real story. Mateo didn't bring a pellet gun to school, did he?"

They sang like birds. Jaylisa, renowned for her loud mouth and array of velour tracksuits, started right in: "Well, you're right there, mister. Mateo didn't think it up himself. Everybody knows he's had a crush on Celeste from the first week of school. Hey, at least he was realistic about who he could get with. Who else did he even have a chance with? But she's so weird, she just totally ignored him."

Tiny, bespectacled, and light-skinned, Philippa chimed in between handfuls of chips, "She don't talk to no one and he can't speak English. Some couple! Also, don't he know Dominicans and Haitians don't mix? He just wanted to get her attention."

"So who gave him the gun?" I asked, trying to appear nonchalant. They paused.

I upped the ante with a packet of sour apple gummy worms. They exchanged "What the hell?" glances and Jaylisa shrugged. "Everybody says it was that bad boy, Sameer. Just doin' it for kicks. Sameer told Mateo if he wanted to get Celeste's attention, he should do something to her—cute-like."

"Cute-like? With a pellet gun?" I asked.

"You know, tease her. Didn't you ever hear that expression, 'Teasing is a sign of love'? Yeah, it was messed up, but it was just a pellet gun. It's not like he was gonna kill her with it."

"What? You use a pellet gun to tease someone? Shooting as a sign of affection?" They ignored my too-obvious questions. As usual, I was the one being schooled.

Jacked up on chili powder and sugar, they giggled and bounded out of the room. "So that's the real deal, mister, but you didn't hear shit from us. We don't want no trouble with that Sameer. Nobody does," Jaylisa said.

Sameer Gherbe. Why hadn't I figured it out myself? It made perfect sense. He was one of the first kids I'd met. He and his mother had come in before the start of school to say they were devout Muslims from Morocco and they were worried about him observing Ramadan during September.

"Do you know Ramadan?" Mrs. Gherbe asked timidly, with a heavy Arabic accent. She had intense dark eyes, a furrowed brow, and seemed older than most of the other mothers.

"Of course," I responded. I explained that with its focus on all things intercultural, the school had plans for a "Ramadan Room" for our observant Muslim students who had to do without food or drink from sunrise to sunset. They could rest when necessary and be away from the temptations of the lunchroom.

"Really?" Mrs. Gherbe gently gathered my hands in hers and stared at me with a gaze so earnest it almost hurt. I started to blush.

"Wonderful!" she cooed.

"I am very happy, you be the teacher of my son," she said. I went on to say I had traveled in their homeland of Morocco.

She turned to her son, who sat quietly beside her. He was a skinny, handsome kid with a halo of dark curls, olive skin, and an infectious "aw, shucks" smile. "Sameer, this man knows our people. He will help you," she said. He nodded and smiled.

In the first weeks of school, it seemed Sameer was spending a *lot* of time in the Ramadan Room, but who was I to judge the pious? I'd never fasted a day in my life. Fish on Fridays during Lent was my only point of reference. After the end of the fast, he started coming to class. Since the year had gotten off to such a bad start, particularly with the boys, I was looking forward to having a male student who was devout and had an involved mother. But like everything else at Union Street, it was a short-lived honeymoon.

A few days after Sameer returned to class, Jim the janitor came into my room. "Hey, Ed, I hate to tell you this, but the teacher in the elementary school on the first floor is really pissed off and wants to talk to you. Something about books flying out the window," he told me. Embarrassed for me, he didn't look up as he methodically swept between the rows of desks.

I ran to the window and looked down in horror to see two copies of *Our Global World*, the new $110 textbook, stewing in a puddle on the blacktop roof several stories below. A Hammond *World Atlas*, its colorful pages flapping wildly in the breeze, had been tossed in for good measure.

Based on the seating chart and my quick grilling of a few students, it became clear that Sameer had thrown our textbooks out the third-story window, and had enlisted two other classmates in his quest. The next morning, Mrs. Gherbe arrived at the principal's office, weepy and despondent. "Sameer is a very good boy" was her sole defense.

Mei delivered swift justice: Sameer and the others would have to pay for the books and faced in-school suspension for three days. "If that book had gone five feet farther, it could have injured or killed some second grader on the sidewalk. How would you feel then?" Mei asked gravely. As Sameer walked out of her office, he looked sufficiently chastened. I was relieved that the incident was being handled with such seriousness.

On my way to lunch the following day, I peered through the tiny window in the principal's office door to see how Sameer was getting along. He was alone, lying on her comfy couch, tossing his head about while listening to his iPod and mouthing lyrics. As an almost absurd extension of the global theme of our school, Mei always had a big maroon bowl of international candies on her desk. They were bizarre-looking and weird-tasting things, shitty-smelling durian-flavored chews from the Philippines and some kind of tamarind taffy from Mexico with a picture of a turkey on it. Judging from the pile of wrappers at his feet, Sameer had apparently made his way halfway around the world. Some punishment. I stormed down the hall and fumed as I told my colleagues about the terms of his "suspension."

Marquis, the tenth-grade history teacher, laughed. "Welcome to Union Street. That's how we roll around here."

During the second day of his suspension, Sameer was busted for smoking pot in a small bathroom near Mei's office. "But it was just a roach!" he protested.

Another quick trial saw him looking impatient while his mother wailed softly in Arabic. This earned him a real suspension for three months, which meant sitting all day with other guilty parties in the now-famous trailer in the Bronx parking lot.

When Sameer returned from the suspension ninety days later, he was angrier and seemingly even more skilled in wreaking havoc. He constantly shadowboxed with unseen enemies; the punches were angry and real, and yet, he still wore that little-boy smile. The other kids were gripped by his stories from his time in suspension, including one about his being stabbed. Swooning girls took turns running their fingers across the red welt on his neck left by the knife.

Sameer had been involved in some minor troubles since his return, but the incident with the pellet gun was serious. So, right after my snack session with Jaylisa and Philippa, I went to Mei and Gretchen with my tip, eager to show them I was more plugged-in than I appeared. They were exhausted by the whole affair and didn't seem eager to discuss it any further.

Gretchen gave a long, exasperated sigh. "Yes, we have heard that version of events secondhand, but we can't get any of them to say Sameer gave Mateo the gun."

"We think he got to all the witnesses before we did and threatened them," Mei said, sounding defeated.

"What can I tell you? That kid is just...sinister," Gretchen added.

That night, I recounted everything to Sam over bowls of leftover ratatouille. I had a mountain of schoolwork to correct, but I couldn't stop fixating on Sameer and the gun incident. I must have sounded like some kind of rabid crank on bad talk radio.

I pounded on the dinner table. "It's killing me that the system failed to get the real bad guy."

"But there's nothing new about that," Sam said. "What is it about this one? It really seems to be getting to you."

As always, he knew me better than I knew myself. I thought about it as I sucked down a third glass of wine. I was drinking a lot those days. It soothed me in the moment, but it messed with my already terrible sleep.

"Until now, I was comforted that there was this kind of unspoken code of honor, a hierarchy, that the thugs didn't mess with the innocents. But now even that is eroding."

He touched the side of my face and looked at me like I was losing it. I was.

"When the monster kids fight each other or even when they beat up on me, it's terrible, but...but watching Celeste and even Mateo really suffer, just for his entertainment...I can't stand that."

Sam talked me through every piece of the story, propping me up, giving me hope, and making me laugh at its absurdities. He pushed aside the piles of work and literally tucked me into bed.

Just as I was about to doze off, the pudgy face of Mateo appeared in my mind. I doubted there was anyone showing him the same kindness in the Baruch housing project. I did what this committed atheist never did and asked the Father, the Son, and begrudgingly even the Holy Fucking Spirit to protect poor Mateo Jimenez in that trailer. I added Celeste to the litany, as well as the other innocents: Fatima, the deeply pious Yemenite girl in a head scarf; and Mo'nique, the chubby girl who seemed to wear the same top every single day—a terrible pilled mint-green sweater. And tiny Lu Huang, too. My lids were getting heavy as I mumbled, "And even that fucker Sameer, don't forget about him, God."

CHAPTER 14

Point of No Return

THE SCHOOL YEAR was heaving its way toward the finish line with drained students and teachers in tow. At the start of almost every period, the kids would tell me exactly how many days we had left until summer vacation. I would act indifferent to their count and, like some cheesy life coach, would say, "That's really unimportant. What matters most is that we stay focused and get a lot done while we are still here. Let's get to work." Behind that facade, I had them all beat at their own game. If they were counting the days, I was marking the minutes.

On the Wednesday of the final week of school, during the last period of the day, I surveyed my classroom. It was hard to see anything but a sad summary of the year before me:

Chivonne had created a miniature beauty shop on her desk. Colorful combs, pins, and a mirror were carefully placed over an unopened (and certainly almost completely blank) notebook. She made no attempt to conceal the contraband or pretend to do her assignment. As she was working some kind of gloppy perfumed product into her hair, I told her to put it all away. Still massaging her scalp with both hands and with a mouthful of pins, she mumbled with indignation, "I can't focus on schoolwork if I don't look good!" She took the pins out of her mouth and got louder: "You always tellin' me to be on time for class. I coulda hid in the bathroom and done this. But no, here I am, in class and on time, and you still wilin'!" By the end of her tirade, she was nearly screaming. "Stop beastin' me, mister. You making me tight." It took another five minutes of back-and-forth for the battle to conclude—yet another entry in a yearlong logbook of wasted time. In room 314, my roles of ineffective cop and feckless social worker always trumped my job as a teacher.

Two desks away sat doe-eyed and petite Angela, the new girl. While I thought I was approaching the limits of compassion as the school year wore on, Angela managed to arouse new sympathy in me. In May, with less than a month of school left, under threat of arrest from a city social worker, Angela's parents brought her from the nearby Baruch housing project to school for the first time all year. Nine months before, at the age of fourteen, just when she should have been starting school, Angela had a baby. But it wasn't her parents' fear of stigma that kept her at home. During her intake interview with Sita, the parents without shame explained in front of their daughter that "school isn't worth it for her since she is practically retarded."

Like Chivonne, she showed a deep focus on an outside project—but this one seemed to involve crayons. I hovered over Angela's desk as she sketched away energetically on a large sheet of pink construction paper cut into the shape of a heart. She was wearing a tight T-shirt and even tighter jeans that pushed her bare post-baby paunch forward for everyone to see. It was jarring to see this on a fourteen-year-old girl, particularly one still playing with crayons, so I glanced at the floor where her neglected notebook sat. I was sure it had even less in it than Chivonne's. On the cover was a proud affirmation in bubbly graffiti-like script: "I ♥ Black Boyz with Big Ones!"

Eager to avoid another public battle, and because I really felt for this kid, I just whispered, "Come on, Angela. This is no time for your art class project or a love letter. You have SO much to do."

She didn't share my interest in keeping the conversation discreet. "Oh don't you worry, mister. This ain't for no art class. I am making a Mother's Day card...for myself." With a wide smile, she held up the card for all to see. She shook her arms for emphasis, revealing that one of her forearms was tattooed with her name in large cursive letters. "I know I'm kinda late for Mother's Day, but I been real busy with the baby." Was she sincere or going for the laugh? I didn't know. My desire to laugh and cry collided in the middle and I just exhaled.

What made the end of the year even more disheartening was that the next fall I was expected to continue with these same kids. World History was a two-year course, and Mei thought "looping," or staying with the same kids for a second year, was better pedagogically. Monica was already sharing lesson plans with me for September, and Gretchen kept talking about new protocols she was eager to try. All this talk of September made me nauseated.

The day was soon over and the kids shuffled out of the classroom with less energy than usual. The June heat had sapped them. I was beat, too, but I set to work reviving my *Jeopardy!* board for a final few days of review. I pulled the huge piece of foam board from my storage closet at the back of the room. My interactions with Chivonne and Angela had already put me in a funk, but seeing that board brought me even lower.

In February, not long after dismissal one day, I had gathered a small group of my advisees in my classroom to help me write a new round of questions for the game. *Jeopardy!* had been a big hit that day and got everyone's competitive juices flowing. Without warning, there was a loud bellowing sound from the hallway. I thought I had heard every kind of noise a teenager could make at that point, but I was wrong. This was a visceral, soul-crushing kind of pain. And then, *CRASH!* as Cesar, a badass sophomore, pounded his fist through the window of my classroom door. The metal meshing embedded in the glass made his terrible wound even worse, opening an artery. Glass sprayed all over my boys and a streak of bright red blood slashed across the *Jeopardy!* board. Stunned, I went to the door and watched as Cesar struggled to pull his twitching limb out of the window. All the blood made me queasy, and I could hear my pulse pounding in my neck. Cesar walked down the hall slowly and in utter silence, his arm limp, slick, and dripping. I should have rushed out to help him. In truth, I was just too damn scared of him and the whole hideous situation. Hiding behind the duty of helping my own kids, I started pulling shards of bloody glass out of the hood of Lu Huang's sweatshirt. Cesar's adviser, Marquis, followed him and Mei ran after with the first-aid kit. I later learned the cause of the uproar: Cesar had been dumped minutes before by a sophomore girl.

Four months later, I looked at the board and could still see remnants of the now-brown blood. I knew what would cheer me up: a visit to my favorite Chinatown food cart to soothe myself with a dollar's worth of greasy pork dumplings. I looked at the clock. If I didn't leave that instant, I knew the cart would be gone and I would miss what was, sadly, the highlight of my day. Just as I was zipping my backpack closed, a surprise visitor sauntered into the room: Chantay. This kid rarely showed up for school lately; what was she doing here *after* school? My dumpling dream would have to be deferred.

She leaned her skinny frame against the bank of windows, cocked her head to the side, and pulled her fingers nervously through her curls. "I gotsta do better, mister. I'm tired of failing. I'm gonna be seventeen next year and still a freshman." Her enormous brown eyes started to fill with tears. It was true: She had a class average of 45, had done almost nothing all term, and had treated me with alternating doses of indifference and disrespect. But I knew she had it rough at home; her plea seemed urgent and sincere. Despite our rocky year, I'd always liked her and admired her spunk. She got to me, and a last-week-of-school conversion was better than none. We sat down together and charted out the things she could do to eke by with a D. I would accept some late assignments during exam week, and she could retake the unit test on Africa. She nodded obediently.

The next day, she showed up for class, where I greeted her like an eager suitor, standing over her with a folder of makeup assignments. But only eighteen hours later, she had other priorities. Rumor had it that she and Jesús were on the rocks. Chantay was flirting up a storm with Javier, another seventeen-year-old freshman. Well-built, handsome, and golden-tongued, he was wearing a red T-shirt that read "The Man, The Myth," and, with a large arrow pointing down to his crotch, "The Legend." There may have been some truth to the claim. Rumor had it that he'd been tossed out of his previous school just a month before, not simply because two girls performed oral sex on him in an empty classroom, but because he had a friend film it on his phone and shared the scene with the world.

I huddled next to Chantay with a folder of earlier assignments and started to review our plan that just might make her a sophomore by age eighteen. In the process, I inadvertently blew her tough-girl cover and let it be known to her peers, including Javier, that she wanted to do some work and pass.

"Chantay, you gettin' your shit together on the down low?" he asked.

"Nah," she purred back at him.

My throat tightened. I was done being played. "So you aren't interested in any of the makeup work we talked about?" I asked.

"What you talkin' about, mister?" she asked, batting her lashes and playing dumb.

I rushed to her desk and snatched the folder back. She turned to Javier and said, "Mister had better get outta my face, or else he gonna get stabbed in his neck." Everybody laughed on cue.

A flare of rage shot through me, which was nothing new, but this time my filter was in the "off" position. I'd be damned if I was going to write up another incident report about her threat. We were on day 175 of a 180-day journey, and I was spent.

"Would anybody guess that Chantay was in here yesterday after school bawling her eyes out, saying that she wanted to pass this class and *finally* be a sophomore? I guess it was all an act." Now I was the one who got the laugh. My adrenaline was flowing as usual in these tense exchanges, but now it was laced with fight, not flight. With the rabble in my corner for once, I went for more. I stuck my face toward hers, drew my lips together snidely, and said in a fake baby voice, "Boo hoo." The kids howled with laughter.

In a flash, Chantay's face instantly went from cocky to pissed-off pouty. "You...you...can't say that. You're a teacher."

"Well, it looks like I just did, don't it?" I said, borrowing the line Kameron had used on me in front of everyone on the first day.

Her tears returned, this time in anger, and she ran out of the classroom. *I'll teach you, you little bitch.* My vengeance felt glorious.

But a minute later, my sobering, inconvenient conscience returned. Rage and sarcasm weren't the answer either. Not even the worst teachers I'd observed, not even Mr. Cooper at Eugene Debs, would have said what I said to her. And I thought I couldn't regress any further.

In the midst of her dramatic exit, I felt my phone vibrating. *Who wants what from me now?* I thought. After the kids filed out of the room, I dialed in to voice mail to hear a message from Helen, my former boss at Project Advance.

"Hi, Ed. I hope all is well with you. I'd love to get together and catch up sometime soon. I have an idea I want to bounce off you." She sounded so cheerful and professional, it was gross.

I had a day off before the start of exams, so I arranged to meet her for breakfast at Cafe Luxembourg, a bistro on the West Side. I approached the table, where the legendarily industrious Helen looked up from a huge pile of paperwork with a wide smile.

In the old days, she and I would often meet with our big donors here. I bounced down onto the leather banquette and felt a familiar ease as I brushed my elbows across the starched linen tablecloth. The waiter brought a basket of buttery French baked goods, which I promptly tore into.

"So, how's it going?" she asked with apparent innocence, though I suspected she had been tipped off to the unfolding disaster by my former coworkers, with whom I'd shared a few of my "worst of" stories over rounds of margaritas. I quickly recapped some of them for her.

Her eyes grew wide and her brow furrowed. "That bad, eh?"

"Yeah, that bad. I just wish I could get to teach. I've got to get a lot meaner. They should require a graduate education course in 'mean.'"

"Are you sure you have a lot of mean in you?"

I thought of my recent diatribe against Chantay. "I'm getting there."

There was a long pause.

"So here's some big news: Louise is leaving us this summer and moving to Boston to get married."

Helen and I had handpicked Louise to be my successor. She was a star who had been on the Project Advance staff when I first arrived and we had wooed her back to take my job.

"Wow, really? How great for her," I said as I cut up a plateful of Salmon Benedict.

"Look"—she stared straight at me—"there's no use in beating around the bush. I invited you here because I want you to come back to your old job."

I hadn't seen this coming. "Really?"

In every shopworn action movie, there is the improbable scene where the protagonist inadvertently uncovers a means of escape just as the zombies are looming, the aliens are invading, or the Nazis are at the door. As Helen made her case for my return, I imagined myself on a sinking ship with waves crashing over the bow. I'm the only one with a life jacket, and I am about to jump off the ship into the last remaining spot in the lifeboat.

"I want you to oversee two other departments as well. I can offer you more money, a better title, and an assistant." Happiness turned to euphoria.

I was just about to say "Yes!" and "When can I start?" when my mind returned to my daydream. Just as I was about to leap off into the lifeboat, I turned to see the panicked faces of my students as the waves crashed around them. They were mouthing words I couldn't understand at first, but they then became clear: "weak," "greedy," "soft." My father, my sisters, my coworkers were on a higher deck with their arms folded, shaking their heads in disapproval. My mother was pointing to the lifeboat, nodding, and smiling from ear to ear.

My yes turned to no in an instant. I pushed my back up against the banquette.

"Helen, that sounds great and I'm flattered, but I can't quit just because it's hard and I'm struggling. I have invested so much in this change, in this decision. I haven't given it enough time. Besides, the principal keeps telling me how much easier the second year is. And she's counting on me to be the grade leader."

"I understand all that. But if you come back, you'll still be helping kids—kids whose talents can make a huge difference."

"I want to help the kids who need it most." My voice became pinched. I wasn't used to emoting in front of Helen.

"If you think you're really helping them, then you should stay and teach," she said. *But am I really helping anyone?* I wondered. Not this year probably, but maybe I could grow into it. Monica and Lindsay had managed to make it work.

"Some days it feels like I'm trying to rescue someone drowning who is pulling me down with them," I told her.

"Well, that sounds pretty awful." She made the sign for the check. "Please think seriously about this. It would be great to have you back. We need you. Good luck with the rest of the year." She gathered up her papers, gave me a peck on the cheek, and walked out of the restaurant.

I pulled on my backpack and walked into a bright June morning feeling full, flattered, and utterly confused.

At long, long last, teaching was over and it was time for State Exam Week. I saw Mei in the teachers' room posting the proctoring schedule on the bulletin board, and found that I'd been assigned to assist Monica with administering and correcting the tenth-grade state history exams that were required by the Board of Regents for graduation. Her students were responsible for two years' worth of material from the World History course—"from Plato to NATO." Monica had taught them history during both ninth and tenth grades in preparation for the big test.

Mei stood over the computer keyboard I was tapping away at. "It will be really helpful for you to proctor and correct these exams, because next year you will have to take your kids through the same gauntlet. It's a really tough test for them. So pay close attention." She had no idea I was thinking of leaving. In the last few weeks, she'd kept promising me how much easier the next year would be.

As I entered the room to monitor the second half of the exam, I recognized a few of Monica's students. I paced up and down the aisles, clacking my shoes against the scuffed linoleum squares. Some kids were scribbling away diligently; others stared blankly at the blackboard. Most looked scared and exhausted as they exited the room as soon as the minimum required time had passed. Only Norris was left. He peered up at me and smiled.

Everyone knew Norris. He was disabled in ways I didn't understand. His head was oddly shaped, and he had a speech impediment and a slight limp. He was also unfailingly kind to everyone. He greeted every teacher every day, even if he wasn't their student. Because he was a Special Ed student, he had unlimited time to complete the exam and stayed more than an hour after the official end time. He handed the exam to me and smiled. I tried not to wince as I scanned his essay, which contained exactly one sentence: "Hitler was a bad man and hurt the good men in Englan n USA." I returned his smile and wished him good luck.

As Norris walked away, I thought about how many of my friends—educated, white, raised in relative privilege—struggled to survive in the city. They had middle-class families and connected friends, and still they struggled to eke out an existence. They couldn't even afford crappy health insurance or to pay their pretty modest student loans. They were hard-pressed to pay rent in Queens, even with five other roommates. If *they* had trouble making it, what were Norris's chances? Who would hire him? House him? Who had Norris's back?

The next day, Monica, Marquis, and I sat in a sweltering classroom correcting the tests. The bulletin boards were now stripped clean and the textbooks had been boxed up. The sounds of liberated kids gleefully roaming the neighborhood below drifted up to our windows. Kid by kid, hour after hour, we pored over the tall stack of exams. We strenuously debated each essay, straining to find every blessed point we could and still preserve our professional integrity.

"Here, where Sherronda writes 'money,' what I think she is really talking about is the free-market system. So, that's five points, right?"

"Does that look like the word 'Rome' to you? I think it is. Partial credit, right?"

"'Famine swept through Europe like a cavity search.' Come on! We can't give credit for that?"

"Here's a memorable one: 'In case you were wondering, this is socialism.'" (It had a cartoon below it with stick figure holding a sickle.)

In a fit of indignation, Monica read a passage from the exam that the students had to comment on.

"'Not only are the peasants compelled to tend the lord's fields, they must also gather manure and chop wood.' How dare they use the word 'manure'! That's so biased against urban kids," she shouted. "They've never even been to a farm."

Try as we might, the kids were no match for the exam. Despite Monica's tremendous efforts, they were lambs before slaughter.

Once the exams were all corrected, we gathered around her to hear the final tally. Silently, Monica tapped on a calculator for a long time and I could see her breaths growing shorter and shorter.

"So, the average score is a"—she squinted downward—"54." Her tone was stoic, but the facade didn't hold. Her shoulders started to shake gently, tears streaming down her face. Then she put her head down on the desk and openly sobbed.

All of us tried to comfort her. "Monica," I pleaded, "I know how disappointed you must be. But come on, without you it would have been an average of 24, and you know it. We all know how far you moved these kids." But she was inconsolable.

Inside, I was dumbstruck. What was I witnessing here? Monica defeated? Crying? Unsuccessful? Monica? All those hours, all those great lessons and creative projects. This is what she had to show for two years of work? A collective 54? (The summer before, a friend who teaches in one of the richest districts in Long Island told me about how disappointed they were if *any* kid got below 85 percent on this exam.)

More than I had realized until that moment, it was Monica who was keeping me in the game. Over the months, I kept consoling myself with a version of this script: *If I really dedicate myself over the next few years, start out really strict, craft great lessons, learn to teach kids to read, put in the hours, I might be half as good as Monica, and that would be plenty good enough.* That story was unspooling in front of me.

In five years, I thought, *will I be sobbing at that same desk?* I admitted to myself what I had been secretly harboring for months: *Maybe most of these kids are too far gone, too hobbled by their life circumstances, for us to help very much.*

I didn't need a roomful of little geniuses like Project Advance, but I needed to feel like some kind of academic progress was being made. Here was my idol, in despair, perched over a pile of yellow exam booklets, blowing her nose and wiping her eyes. It was more frightening than watching the most violent, ruthless behavior from the kids.

I said a few more kind words to Monica and went to the bathroom to try to steady myself. I stood in front of the mirror blotting my face and talking myself down loudly. I didn't care who heard. "Make up your mind now, Eddie. Go where you'll make the biggest difference and be happy. Enough with the goddamn martyr complex." It all came down to that single minute.

I bounded down the stairs of the Union Street School three at a time and darted out into the June heat of the Lower East Side. I ran to a corner, starting to sweat through my shirt, and pulled out my phone. My head was swollen with sadness and regret, but there was also the aching anticipation of freedom, of release. I dialed my old boss quickly, fearing I would change my mind.

"Helen, it's Ed. I've been thinking about that job. As long as you promise not to stab me in my neck, I'll come back to work at Project Advance."

I walked into the school the next morning. Without the kids there, it was so quiet I hardly recognized it as the same place. I found Mei and Gretchen in the main office and told them my decision. They were polite, even congratulatory about my new job, and probably not surprised. They both looked so spent at that point in the year it was hard to know what they really felt. Many other teachers, some of them very gifted educators, had announced their departures over the last few weeks. I went home and called Nora and told her my news sheepishly. She seemed relieved for me. When I called my mother she said, "Well, I'm glad you got that out of your system. That's great about your new job."

They were short conversations, everyone eager for my embarrassment to end, but as I look back, here is what I wanted to tell them all. I'd have to leave the *To Sir, with Love*; *Stand and Deliver*; and

Blackboard Jungle endings to the Hollywood heroes and the super-human twenty-two-year-olds who are made of stronger stuff than I am. My god, how I wished I were tougher, more resilient, more organized, harder working, and less in love with bourgeois pleasures, but I was not, am not. I have reenacted every fight, insult, and outburst but cast each scene with a better version of myself as a veteran teacher, and I always emerge victorious. But would it really have worked? Would it have made a difference?

I still wrestle with flashes of guilt, shame, and betrayal. A white guy with a salvation complex is bad enough, but how about one who couldn't save anybody? Every time I walk by a school or see a band of rowdy kids on the subway, these demons revisit me. I so wish it were a different ending for me and for the kids, but some stories have to end like a seventies movie—gritty, real, and sad.

Chapter 15

Pomp and Circumstance

The fact remains that getting people right is not what living is all about anyway. It's getting them wrong that is living, getting them wrong and wrong and wrong and then, on careful reconsideration, getting them wrong again. That's how we know we're alive: we're wrong. Maybe the best thing would be to forget being right or wrong about people and just go along for the ride. But if you can do that—well, lucky you.

—Philip Roth, *American Pastoral*

THREE YEARS AFTER I left the Union Street School, sometime in late June 2010, I banged out a few final e-mails in my office, pulled off my tie, and bounded down the stairs of the Project Advance brownstone located on a leafy block on the Upper West Side. I hopped on my dinged-up, mint-green Bianchi cruiser and headed downtown through a snarled mess of yellow cabs, rolling hot-dog carts, and defiant pedestrians. After a frantic ride, I arrived at a small, dark auditorium somewhere on the NYU campus, just in time for the Union Street graduation ceremony.

The early summer heat and the anxiety of seeing my former students in the flesh left me short of breath as I grabbed a program and plopped down in a squeaky fold-down seat. Up until that point, with a notable exception or two, I had purposely avoided much interaction with the school or its students. Eager to put the ugly year behind me, I had thrown myself into my position at Project Advance with renewed conviction. I was more partisan than ever about the program, believing that low-income kids with the greatest promise are well served in private schools, where their talents can be cultivated and they have the best chance of joining the leadership class.

I watched as my former students filed onto the stage, beaming and mugging in shiny green graduation robes with their mortarboards askew. They took up surprisingly little of the stage. I did a quick count and was saddened to discover that only about half of the original class of ninety students would be graduating; the missing could be chalked up to dropouts, expulsions, and transfers. As I scanned the rows of faces, I was hard-pressed to believe that several of those onstage had really met the state graduation requirements, which had grown even more rigorous since I had left. My suspicion was later confirmed by shrugs and rolled eyes from faculty members.

Lucas, the brainy son of Haitian immigrants and one of the few middle-class kids in the school, gave a moving commencement speech, urging his classmates to make their mark on the world. It also featured a walk down memory lane, including a reference to "terrible fights inside Mr. Boland's classroom," which left the graduates laughing and my face burning with embarrassment. Always right behind Byron in terms of grades, Lucas concluded by saying he would attend Vassar in the fall. As happy as I was for him, he was very much the exception. Those kids going on to higher education were mostly headed to community colleges, and even then it was largely through remedial programs.

At the reception afterward, to my great surprise I was swarmed by students like some kind of celebrity, by kids who formed a sort of receiving line. Even more shocking was the fact that I was most warmly received by the students who had seemed to hate and resist me the most.

For the entire year I taught her, Gloria Lin didn't make eye contact with me and mumbled insults under her breath, sometimes in Cantonese, sometimes in English. Here, she held me in a long bear hug, saying, "You were an amazing history teacher! Why did you leave?" Even three years later, the mindfuck continued.

"Mister, mister, look at my beautiful baby girl," said DiNatalya. She hadn't graduated that afternoon but had come to cheer on her classmates. She frantically thumbed through her phone and brought up pictures of a cherubic six-month-old crowned with a wisp of black hair. I congratulated her but thought about how hard the road ahead would be for someone with her challenges. I wanted to cry.

José, whom I remembered as a smart-mouth with terrible grades, was next. "I'm goin' to JTC College an' study international business," he said. I slapped him on the back and shook his hand. Inside, I was fuming. I knew it was one of those sinister for-profit colleges, which lure in the weakest students with deceptive, cynical advertising: "Be somebody!" "Do it for yourself and your kids!" "No high school diploma necessary!" They're expensive and they load their students up with taxpayer-funded loans and grants, but 63 percent of the kids drop out because they are so unprepared. In the end, the schools keep the money (one CEO of a chain of for-profit colleges, Strayer Education, Inc., made $41.9 million in 2009), but students rarely get the degrees promised and they are stuck with a mountain of debt.

Dalia, whose name I barely remembered since her attendance was so terrible, embraced me. "Mister, I got some more high school courses to do, but when I finish I'm gonna join the Marines, just like my dad." I'm all for serving your country, but I knew she had few other options. I took a picture with her and forced out another smile.

But there was real cause for celebration, too: Manfred, one of the students who had held his own with Byron and Lucas, earned nearly a full scholarship to Pace University to study business. (He sends me his good news from time to time. He went on to graduate with a degree in environmental science, studied abroad in Hong Kong, and just landed a great job working for an eco-conscious leather producer.) Ahmed would go to Baruch College to study computer science. Even more encouraging, several of the middle-of-the-pack kids took unexpected turns for the good: Dee-Dee, a quiet, unmoti-vated, sometimes surly girl, blossomed as a spoken-word artist and earned a near full-ride scholarship to the very groovy Hampshire College, where I was sure the hippies and hipsters would love her. Lazy Lee Lee turned it on somewhere along the way and would go on to study economics at St. John's in Queens.

I said my final good-byes, exchanged e-mail addresses with a few kids, and unchained my bike from a light post. As I started pumping my way back uptown, my mood shifted at almost every intersec-tion. I felt alarmed for those missing, concerned for those exploited, and overjoyed for the steady workhorses and turnaround artists. So much for neat closure.

Since graduation day, largely through the wonders of e-mail, Facebook, and gossip, I have tried to stay connected to my former students and colleagues.

Mei and Gretchen both left (or were forced out, depending on who you talk to) the school not long after I did. Mei was promoted to the Academic Office of the Department of Education, where she evaluates the performances of schools like the one she left. Gretchen moved on to a big job at an educational nonprofit that supports teachers and principals and opens new reform-minded schools. (Mei's replacement as principal, Meghan, was widely disliked by the faculty, and a significant exodus ensued. She left in 2012 for a senior administrative post in teacher "talent management" in a big school district out west.) Union Street School is now on its third principal since its founding in 2004.

In August 2012, New York State declared Union Street a "priority school," meaning it was performing in the bottom 5 percent of schools statewide. Not surprisingly, Eugene Debs is also on that list, but it was especially disheartening to see that Union Street underperformed even Eugene Debs in terms of math and English scores. It was mandated that Union Street dramatically improve its performance or face closure by 2015. Only 10.2 percent of students were reported as having met state standards in English, and a mere 10 percent of the seniors were classified as "college ready." It is hard to square these sad facts with the school's tagline: "College Ready. Globally Competent." It is unclear how the new and more union-friendly administration of Mayor Bill de Blasio will deal with such schools.

I know Mei, Gretchen, and Meghan were smart, well-intentioned, and worked extremely hard. I know that society unfairly expects educators to fix larger societal problems through schools, but it's disconcerting that the school's early leaders have been promoted up the chain despite terribly poor results.

All but two of the thirty-two faculty members I taught with at Union Street have either moved on to other schools or left the profession. One year after I left, Monica went on to Harvard Business School. After graduating, she tried corporate management consulting but disliked it. She is now back working for the largest school district in the Midwest, overseeing school performance, trying to fix the big machine. If anyone can do it, she can. Bridget, the science teacher, got fed up with teaching and moved to the United Arab Emirates for a time. Last I heard, she was running an organic beet farm in upstate New York. My buddy Porter, who taught ninth-grade English, stayed for four years at Union Street, but then in frustration moved to a new school that attracts more motivated kids and focuses on creative writing. In June 2014, he saw his new school's first-ever graduating class go on to some excellent colleges. The social worker, Sita, went on to do God's work in a school for recently incarcerated youth. Her stories are legend. A student told her recently, "Miss, this morning I robbed this lady that looked like you, but she had money."

Rebecca, the charismatic middle school reading teacher at Union Street, eventually become the principal of a reasonably well-regarded high school in Queens. In 2014, she was escorted out of the school by investigators, accused of having had sex with both a school security guard and a vice principal—in school, during school hours. Photos of her having sex (including a three-way tryst) were reportedly found on school computers; the ones of her in lingerie soon made their way to the *New York Post*; even newspapers in England and China covered the story. A student's father, with whom she was romantically involved at the time, alerted authorities to the situation. Even though she was wildly out of line, it's still a terrible loss of talent.

As for the kids, Chantay, who greeted me during my first week with some serious profanity, finished her associate's degree at a community college in upstate New York and has transferred to a four-year state college on Long Island. She doesn't really like it that much and plans to take the NYC police officer exam or go to culinary school soon. Kameron, aka "Nemesis," who was suspended for threatening to blow up the school, later attended a high school for "post-incarceration and juvenile detention center youth." It's hard not to assume the worst about why he ended up there. Bad boy Jesús, who participated in the rumble along with his father, posts on Facebook about wanting to join the Navy SEALs, but also about how he's going to "get lifted with this blunt before my GED class." The empty lot that hosted the rumble is on the verge of total gentrification. Essex Crossing will be one of the largest developments in New York in decades, consisting of nearly two million square feet of shops and apartments. The neighborhood is quickly becoming unrecognizable.

The fate of Freddy, who was running a drug ring in his brother's absence, is unclear, but I am sad to report that there was a prisoner with his name and year of birth in an upstate New York prison who served eighteen months for possession of a controlled substance. Sameer, the textbook thrower and pellet-gun provider, went to community college for a time and lists his profession on Facebook as "your mother's massage therapist." He is a pretty good boxer. I ran into him on the subway recently. He again showed me a long, fat worm of a scar on his neck. "Chicks like to suck on it," he reminded me. He asked me to take him and a friend out for beers, but I politely declined. Mickey, the bad boy of Temple Emmanu-El fame, continued his scorched-earth policy during his sophomore year until finally he slammed Mei up against a wall and was permanently expelled. Even his grandmother couldn't explain that one away. He attended a "second-chance" high school in East Harlem but didn't graduate and is now unemployed. We chat on Facebook from time to time. He says he's "chillin' and tryin' to stay out of trouble."

Valentina, of Kingda Ka roller-coaster fame, is studying to become either a heart surgeon or a manicurist, depending on which of her Facebook posts you believe. But later she told me in an e-mail that she had dropped out of a medical technician training program at a for-profit trade school. She found it "overwhelming" and said "u have to keep up on everything because it's not like community college, it's hard." She hopes to reenroll in the program soon. She was recently arrested and spent five days in jail on Rikers Island. She celebrated her release by getting "white girl drunk." She will soon have a baby. Aspirational Solomon is in community college in the Bronx studying criminal justice in the hopes of becoming a cop, and also working at Staples. I don't know if Leon came out of the closet, but he was, until recently, working as a florist of sorts, creating elaborate edible fruit arrangements. Mariah, who does maintenance work in parks, is no longer quiet about her sexuality. She recently declared on Facebook that "I'm addicted to FEMS. Want A Boo So I Could Lay Up with Her And Rub Her Butt." Fat Clovis is happily married and working at a Walmart in Tennessee and seems his blithe self. Yvette, who was sexually exploited and loved *Powers of Ten*, is nowhere to be found.

By the time he was a senior, Byron had aced every course at Union Street and had only two hours of class a day; there were no honors or AP courses offered there. With the help of a really dedicated teacher, he taught himself some very advanced math topics. Since the school wasn't well suited to help him with his applications to competitive colleges, I stepped in as a volunteer college counselor. Despite his impeccable record, stellar scores, and compelling story, his undocumented (I refuse to use the word *illegal*) immigration status made him a hard sell to colleges. Undocumented students are ineligible for federal financial aid, so a school would have to fill the gap with their own funds to enroll him, and those funds are usually reserved for international students who live abroad.

On the big decision day, Byron was wait-listed at Harvard,

Brown, and Kenyon. I tried to use my connections at all three schools to move him off the list, but to no avail. One admissions officer told me, "It's not looking good. We'll treat him as a foreign student, but we only have four spots in the entire class for full-scholarship foreign students. He's got stiff competition." I knew from my former jobs in college admissions the kinds of kids he was competing with: former child soldiers from Sierra Leone, Indian whiz kids who've done research on malaria drugs, Chinese prodigies who have written their own math theorems.

We brainstormed a backup plan for him to attend boarding school for a postgraduate year while he got his citizenship status straightened out. I called just about every boarding school in the Northeast, but it was already June so the classes were filled and the financial aid was gone. Only a third-tier Catholic boarding school in Massachusetts that used to educate the lesser Kennedys showed interest. I took a day off and we drove to the campus. Byron was impressed by the rolling hills, the Gothic campus, and the seriousness of the students. Later that week, I called him with the news of a nearly full scholarship. There was an awkward silence on the line and he finally blurted out, "I appreciate your help in getting me this, but I don't want to go. I don't want to be eighteen and wear a uniform and have a curfew." It was hard to know if I was more furious or sad at his self-sabotage. Was he afraid of failure? Of success? Was he secretly scared of all those blondes swinging squash racquets? I would never know.

Later that year, Byron moved to rural Florida where, because of his undocumented status, he was unable to work or get financial aid for college. He has done very little of anything except go to the public library and help his aunt sell meat pies from time to time. In the fall of 2012, Byron was given a glimmer of hope. The federal government offered a temporary amnesty from deportation program called DACA (Deferred Action for Childhood Arrivals) that allows students who were brought to this country by their parents to work and receive federal aid legally. He applied, was approved, and now plans to reapply to college. I hope our nation will do right by hard-working kids like Byron. The old slogan has never rung more true: "A mind is a terrible thing to waste."

I have also stayed in touch with Nee-cole, the girl in foster care who was bullied by her classmates. Her homeless but savvy mother had her transferred to a better public school after one year at Union Street. From time to time, I would see her mother tasting samples of vegan products at Whole Foods and we'd catch up on Nee-cole. Though nationally only 2 percent of children in foster care earn college degrees, remarkably, Nee-cole just graduated from a competitive four-year state college in Westchester in a special program that supports at-risk kids. Her experience has been filled with low lows and high highs. I checked in with her during the early days of her freshman year and discovered that without a computer, she was writing her papers on her cell phone when the library was closed, and her foster care agency was six weeks late with a check for books. Sam and I did what we could, buying her a used computer and sending her money for textbooks and to keep her phone from being turned off. True to her character, she would accept only a loan, not a gift, and repaid me the minute her check arrived. At one point, she failed several courses and was put on academic probation.

But there have been good times, too. After I hadn't seen her for almost a year, we caught up over lunch in her junior year, slurping noodles at a ramen joint on Broadway. I was afraid she might be close to dropping out. Instead, she laid the news on me: "I got a 3.3 GPA for the semester and I wanted to thank you for all your encouragement. I hope you like this." She handed me a box, and inside was a carefully folded navy blue sweater, which turned blurry as my eyes welled up. I was elated. Afterward, to celebrate her accomplishment, we sat side by side getting pedicures and gossiping about the bad old days and the mean girls of Union Street.

No matter how you cut it, the academic results of Union Street, a reform-minded school that endeavored to prepare students for college, were poor. Of the roughly ninety freshmen I taught in 2006, I am in touch with more than half. Of those, only three students I know of graduated from a four-year college in a four-year period.

In fairness to the former Bloomberg administration, which championed the small schools movement, Union Street's results are well below average. Overall, this change to the system is standing the test of time. In 2014, a major multiyear study of twenty-one thousand NYC students in small schools showed a nearly 10 percent higher graduation rate than in large schools. The results are particularly striking for young black men who graduated from New York's small schools: They enrolled in college at a rate of just over 43 percent; that may sound horrific, but it beats the big high schools by more than 10 percent.

A year after the Union Street graduation, I found myself again in the Grand Ballroom of the Waldorf Astoria. Another full-capacity crowd had gathered for the Project Advance gala honoring another Wall Street titan. As always, I moved through the crowd thanking the donors, but tonight it was hard not to be struck by another group of people in the room: the accomplished alumni of the program whom I saw at every turn. I had a happy reunion with Sharon, the young woman who inspired my decision to teach at that same event in the same room years before. I remembered her words from 2004 vividly: "Take the plunge, Ed. Go and teach." After Choate, she excelled at Harvard and then Columbia Law School. She earned two prestigious clerkships and is now a lawyer at one of the most prestigious white-shoe firms in New York. She is one of Project Advance's 263 lawyers. Next, I spotted Jaime, an eye surgeon, one of the program's one hundred doctors, who'd recently been appointed to the Yale Medical School faculty. I had observed him in surgery the month before, when he restored the sight of a thirteen-year-old girl with a rare condition. Nearby stood Nate, a recent Brown graduate who postponed his dream of getting a PhD in paleontology to open a charter school in East New York, Brooklyn, one of the lowest academically performing districts in the country. An alum who is a special assistant to President Obama for Legislative Affairs was there, as well as the program's first White House Fellow.

After a last-minute pep talk before the dinner, I sent Julia, a high school senior, to the podium. She had been chosen to share her journey with the crowd. Brilliant, modest, and polished, Julia was the oldest of four daughters raised in the Bronx by a strict, single Dominican mother. She opened with a confession: Knowing how overprotective her mother was, five years before, she forged her mother's signature to apply to Project Advance and then again on her application to boarding school in Massachusetts. Julia excelled at boarding school and, among a slew of other honors and awards, was voted the top freshman girl by the faculty. As if the crowd weren't enthralled enough, she ended with this:

"This spring, I called my mother to give her some amazing news. 'Mami, *me aceptaron en* Harvard!!' I yelled as soon as she picked up the phone. There was an awkward pause. 'Okay,' she said, 'don't stay up too late tonight, *adios*,' and she hung up the phone. Wasn't she happy for me? Proud of me? Then it hit me. My mother had never heard of Harvard."

Then 150 more seniors, each headed to an impressive college, joined Julia onstage. The crowd leaped to its feet and applauded for a solid five minutes.

This event has always been the highlight of my year and yet, without warning, I felt a pang of sadness. Even years after my failed foray at teaching, so much of me wished that this were the Union Street graduation I was witnessing. That I was watching my former students cross the stage on their way to great colleges and bright futures.

While this isn't the story I was hoping to tell, despite it all, I have made my peace and remain defiantly hopeful. I realize that all steps forward, whether halting and small or bounding and grand, are valuable. I am as proud of Nee-cole as I am of Julia. Encouragement, good role models, and the occasional break can open a whole new world for a kid. And conversely, with a few wrong turns and without the right opportunities and support, any kid can end up robbed of a promising future.

Any role I have played in a young person's life—no matter how direct or indirect—during my decade at Project Advance or, yes, even during my dismal year at Union Street, is a worthy one. As I walked out of the ballroom and into the cacophony of Lexington Avenue, it hit me: I'd be a fool not to celebrate where I am and what I have tried to do.

A Message to Charles

It was January 2013, six months after the benefit at the Waldorf, on the kind of dark winter evening when 5:30 p.m. feels like the dead of night. Snow flurries plinked lightly against the windows of a downtown loft space where a Project Advance trustee was holding a reception for our undergraduates interested in careers in education.

Representatives from all the big teaching recruitment programs and charter schools were in the room eagerly trying to attract Project Advance's college seniors. For them, this was a mother lode: Instead of the usual surfeit of well-intentioned, upper-middle-class white kids eager to help the urban poor, here was a roomful of brilliant, pedigreed students of color who looked like and had lived like the kids they would teach.

I was engaged in an awkward conversation with one of them: Charles Lee, a supersweet super nerd I'd known since he entered the program in fifth grade. A self-described "über-mutt," he was a mix of Caribbean black and Hakka Chinese by way of Jamaica with some Bronx Puerto Rican thrown in for good measure.

"It's really important for me to give back, and there's no question that teaching is the best way to do it." Small-boned and earnest, Charles looked up from a plate piled high with waxy, precut cubes of yellow and white cheese, which he was devouring as only a college kid could. He gulped down another piece and continued. "Being part of Project Advance, attending private school, and having all these advantages opened my eyes to just how unfair the whole educational system really is. I want to make a difference."

I nodded. His words were eerily familiar. It was practically the same "into the fray of teaching" spiel that I'd given everyone several years earlier.

"So, Mr. Boland, tell me about your experience. I *know* they loved you! Lots of lightbulbs going off over everybody's heads, I bet." During graduate school, I'd served as a teaching assistant in Charles's history class during the academic boot camp that all Project Advance kids must undergo for fourteen months before private school. Now he was five months away from graduating from Brown with honors in economics. The investment banks were falling all over themselves to snatch this kid up, but his first priority was to do something altruistic. A charter school network representative had just spent the last half hour giving him the hard sell, and he seemed close to signing on the dotted line for a two-year stint in an underserved Brooklyn school.

I strained a fake smile. "Well, sure...there were lightbulbs going off...now and again."

He looked a little puzzled.

"Did you feel well supported by your school?"

"Yeah, to an extent. There were some things in place."

"Well, all the programs and schools that I'm considering have a lot of special supports for new teachers."

"I am sure they do." I latched my teeth onto the lip of a plastic wine tumbler and thought back to the "special support" meetings at Union Street that were promised for new teachers. We ended up having a total of two: the first one two days before the start of school and the second after about a week of classes. At the first meeting, I remember the powerful words of a new middle school math teacher, Althea, a bougie, twenty-two-year-old, oft-proclaimed Christian, right out of Howard University. She spoke about the special responsibility she felt to give back to poor communities of color before she went off to graduate school. We were all so moved by her words. Only ten days later, at the second meeting, she was bawling her eyes out, pounding on a desk, and howling about her students: "They are *ANIMALS!*" We sat in stunned silence. Next to her was the new Spanish teacher, Alvin, who was right out of Tufts. He lasted a month before he threw in the towel. Some support.

"Did you feel like you were making a difference?" Charles asked.

"Look, Charles, I'll level with you. It was a tough year. I had a hard time with classroom management," I said, churning inside with ambivalence. I had returned to a world where I was confident and successful, and I didn't like being dragged back to the clusterfuck of Union Street.

"You only stayed...a year?" His smile disappeared and his shoulders dropped a little.

"But it'll be different for you," I sputtered. "You're tougher than I am." It was a stretch: Charles weighed 120 pounds soaking wet; his voice was slight and reedy. At least there was six feet of me to abuse. I feared they would eat him alive.

"I don't consider myself very tough," he said.

"Well, you'll get tough!" I said, just a little too loud. I was trying to be honest but encouraging; I was being neither.

"As much as I want to teach, I also think investment banking would be interesting, and I could really help out my parents financially. So what do you think, Mr. Boland, should I try teaching?"

I pretended not to hear his question, waved to someone, and

started to the other side of the room. "Good luck with your decision. I really should say hi to a few other people."

In the following weeks, I returned repeatedly to my conversation with Charles. Ashamed of my evasion, I thought long and hard about his question. I started writing him an e-mail but was never satisfied with its message. I saved draft after draft, each one growing longer and more ambitious. Finally, late one night, months after seeing him, after two whiskeys and a shot of espresso, I hit Send on my e-mail message with the subject line, "Ramblings from a One-Year Flameout." Below is a modified and fortified version of what I sent him:

Dear Charles,

Great to see you at the education reception in January. I'm afraid I owe you an apology. That evening you asked me if you should try teaching. In the moment, I lacked the courage and clarity to offer you an honest answer, but since then I have given your question a great deal of thought. Like most educational exchanges, I learned more in putting this "lesson" together than you will in reading it. I suppose that's the first secret of the business: Teachers are always taught far more by their students than the reverse.

Before I launch in, let me say a word about why I feel qualified to answer at all. Where do I—a product of nearly total parochial education, professionally steeped in elite educational institutions, and with only one disastrous year of public school teaching under my belt—get off giving you advice? Well, to be blunt, most of the wisdom of the experts I read in graduate school (from the left, right, and center politically, and from those who shuffle between all three camps) and advice I heard from my school administrators was not helpful. I am by no stretch an expert, but I can offer you what I wished I'd heard as I was making my decision to teach and what I've gleaned from two decades of working in different educational settings. So from my admittedly limited vantage point, here is my answer:

My answer is: "Yesbut," and the "but" is pretty big because it is likely going to be brutally hard on you emotionally, physically, and intellectually. Do it! Go and teach your heart out. Teach those little monsters till it hurts—and it will. In the hopes of making it sting a little less, here, in no particular order, is my advice for a first-year teacher in a tough school:

Scrutinize Your Prospective Schools

In retrospect, if I had done more homework, I would have taken a job I was offered at a gem of a small high school in Brooklyn that serves the same type of students as Union Street, but with a more cohesive and disciplined approach and far better results.

Like me, you'll encounter a bustling marketplace of reform ideas, each sounding more promising than the last. It's easy for a novice to be duped by a sales pitch or get the wrong impression in a quick afternoon visit to a school, so be on the lookout for any warning signs. Ask hard questions to find out if those ideas are making a difference. If you do your homework, you will go in with your eyes wide open and hopefully find a school with a philosophy that matches your personality and passions.

First, look at the hard data. There is more public information about school performance available today than ever before, but it is often hard to locate and interpret. Do the legwork to gather information from a variety of sources—official and unofficial. Read every website, survey, and evaluation you can find. Don't just look at standardized test scores, but delve into class size, school safety surveys, student and teacher attendance, number of suspensions, percent of English Language learners and Special Ed students, staff turnover percentage, graduation rates, and college/career readiness measures. While there are no magic numbers that will ensure success, look at how schools with similar student bodies compare.

Second, gather your own impressions while visiting: What is the caliber and type of work being asked of the students? What kinds of questions are the kids asking? Has their curiosity been piqued or are they just following orders? Do teachers appear to share an educational philosophy? How do the teachers and the administration interact? Don't just ask the administrators; if possible, find opportunities to question current and past teachers, parents, students and alumni, grad school professors and classmates.

Third, seek out a principal who is both visionary and practical, someone who can quote the curriculum gurus and get the cell phone out of a kid's hand in three seconds flat. (Think half Steve Jobs, half Captain Queeg.) My school and administration were driven by progressive ideas and dedicated to reform, but without discipline the kids ran amok and little was accomplished. Other schools are run with military discipline and precision, but lack educational vision and warmth.

Is Everyone on the Same Page with Classroom Management?

During a nasty battle over gum chewing with a student one day, she complained to me, "Half of you teachers will let me chew and half of you won't. Why don't you just make up your minds?" She was right. Students shouldn't have to learn a different set of rules and consequences for each of their seven teachers. It confuses them and violates their sense of what is right. Look for evidence of behavioral norms and expectations across classrooms. Is there a philosophy that permeates the school? Teachers should be largely using the same language and following the same procedures to manage their classrooms for everything from small infractions to the most serious suspensions. That consistency tells students there is a right way to act.

But, as important, whatever that classroom management philosophy is, make sure that you are comfortable following it. If you are not willing to enforce utterly straight lines in the hallway all day long, don't choose a school where that is part of the culture. If being a "no excuses" badass is required, make sure you are a bit of a badass; otherwise, students will smell the insincerity a mile away. They know "frontin'" when they see it. If the setting is more progressive and long, reflective psychosocial conversations with students about their behavior are the norm, make sure you have the mettle for that as well.

Doug Lemov's Teach Like a Champion *is the kind of teacher's bible I wish had existed when I taught. Its power is in its specificity to describe and rationalize teaching and behavioral techniques. (He even tells teachers there is a right way to stand still!) In retrospect and at the risk of oversimplifying, I realize being consistent, calm, clear, and positive with my off-task students would have been far more effective than my default: loud, fast, angry, and grasping for a different system of discipline every month.*

Two final words of advice about classroom management that I heard too late from great teachers: Resist the urge to resent and withdraw from the kids who fight you the hardest; they are the ones who need you the most. Tell yourself your most nightmarish student is your favorite and act like it. And second, don't be afraid to admit publicly to kids when you have made a mistake. You'll gain credibility and respect, and they'll respond in kind.

Plan Every Minute, Plan Every Detail

The nuns who taught me in grammar school had it right: "An idle mind is the devil's playground." If students sense there is a highly structured classroom culture in place, they will focus more and act out less. I paid the price for failing to create classroom systems and procedures from the beginning. Figure out exactly when and how a student can sharpen a pencil, request to use the bathroom, and answer a question. Do seating charts. Post signs clarifying the rules. Create a system of rewards and consequences for good and bad behavior. But here's the even harder part: Once the system is in place, consistent enforcement is key. All of us respond to consistency, but children especially so. Make it clear to students that full engagement is required from the minute they walk over your threshold to the second they pack up. Overprepare your lessons to make sure there is no downtime. Go the extra mile to make your lesson plans more engaging; even the most tedious topics can be enhanced with a little creative flair.

Find Dedicated Mentors; Milk Them for All They're Worth
The mentoring program for new teachers at Union Street was sporadic and ever-changing, so I sought out my own mentor in Monica. If a school has a more formalized mentoring program it can be tremendously beneficial, but it's no guarantee if the match isn't right. As a seasoned dean of students once told me, "Latch on to the teacher whose classroom makes you feel right at home, the person who looks most like your aspirational teacher-self. Stalk them. Flatter them. Observe them frequently. Have them observe you constantly." In retrospect, I wish I had asked twice as many questions of the informal mentors I found and asked for help three times more often. Also, if possible, find another veteran outside of the school community to whom you can occasionally vent, cry, and rant without fear of repercussions in your workplace. My sister Nora played that role for me, and it was tremendously helpful.

Pamper Alert: Take Care of Yourself

Find hobbies, sports, indulgences, favored substances, and some kind of therapy that will get your head out of the game when you need a break. Build them into your schedule; otherwise, you will never do them. Eat well, get enough sleep, and take power naps after school. As you plan your weekly lessons, build in specific downtime for yourself. Martyrs burn out early and hard, and that doesn't help anyone. My Wednesday-night volleyball games were a lifesaver.

Yesbut

I have given you the "yes" in my "yesbut," but now brace yourself for the "but," because it is daunting. Without a doubt, by teaching you can help close the educational achievement gap in a real and palpable way. You will touch lives and make an enormous difference. However, as hard as you will work and as much as you will devote yourself to your new profession, you need to recognize from the outset just how much of the entire enterprise is determined outside of your classroom and ultimately outside of your control. No sustained and widespread change will come about until and unless we address the broader problems in our educational system and the even larger, looming societal challenges. It's a long list of structural woes: poverty, institutional racism, and deep flaws in the way we design, run, and pay for our school systems. I warn you about these external forces not to discourage you, but so that you will see your frequent setbacks as emanating from causes beyond your power and count your victories, as small as they might be, as causes for celebration.

I'll end my rant here, Charles, and simply say: Go forth and give it your all.

With great respect,
Ed

*   *   *

Through Teach For America, Charles went on to teach third grade at a charter school in Brownsville, one of the lowest academically performing neighborhoods in New York. Because he lacked experience, he was initially made an assistant teacher to a ten-plus-year veteran who had just been recruited from a high-performing public school in suburban Ohio, but she had little experience in teaching underserved kids. They chewed her up and spit her out in three weeks' time and Charles was promoted to head teacher. Against the odds and despite my pessimism, he took control of the classroom and did an admirable job: The test scores of his students in English increased by 50 percent and even more in math.

His is a story that gives us hope as much as mine discourages us. But here's the rub: Tales of individual teacher and school success and failure serve as a dangerous distraction for those who care deeply about changing the trajectory of American education. To enact real change, we must step outside the system and stop expecting schools and teachers alone to create lasting solutions.

This is a call to radical action for elected officials at all levels, academics, union heads, private sector leaders, and, most important, ordinary citizens to take up this cause. Here are the most pressing priorities that we as a society must embrace to reform our broken and unfair educational system:

INTEGRATE SCHOOLS

After decades of progress, we have returned to an educational system of severe racial segregation. Today's students of color attend schools with fewer white students than they did in the 1960s.

Integrated schools are not simply a comforting democratic affirmation that children can learn and play together; decades of research have shown that the practice actually results in higher achievement for lower-income students. Recent studies have shown that a school's racial composition may have an even greater effect on student achievement than family background. It may be even more effective (and cost-efficient) than in-school reforms such as a longer school day, the ability to fire teachers, and curricular innovations. With careful policy choices and greater political finesse, we can avoid past unsuccessful attempts at integration. Practices that work to expand the number of desirable schools rather than simply promote competition for seats in good schools will avoid white flight to suburban districts and to parochial/private alternatives.

RETHINK SCHOOL FUNDING

Despite the fact that the United States spends more money by far on public education than any other country on earth, it doesn't spend those funds equitably. We spend it worse than equitably, we disadvantage the poor by design: Unlike almost every other developed country, we actually favor the students who have more resources over students with less. It is exactly the opposite of what common sense and fair-mindedness dictate. Much of the underlying problem is that the majority of school expenses in the United States are funded by local property taxes. The practice encourages self-interested enclaves of privilege and promotes neighborhood segregation. For example, even in a progressive state like New York, the affluent town of Southampton spends over $39,000 per pupil, and the Rust Belt city of Utica spends $14,600. Other states like Illinois have even greater per-pupil spreads, ranging from $5,000 to $28,000. Since the 1960s, scores of lawsuits brought by advocacy groups and unions have begun to slowly chip away at the gap, but the pace of change has been glacial and the implementation uneven. Federal and especially state governments must be held accountable to level the playing field.

INVEST MORE IN THE RESEARCH, DEVELOPMENT, AND EVALUATION OF EDUCATION

In the great American debate over how we should spend more than $550 billion a year on education, there is one priority that is all too often given short shrift: funding for creating and testing what truly works in education reform. (We spend less than 1 percent of educational dollars on R & D; most applied fields spend somewhere between 10 and 15 percent.) Before billions of dollars and millions of students and teachers are subjected to new curricula and pedagogy, reforms and technology, government in concert with universities must ensure that they are effective by conducting larger, longer-term, and more rigorous studies. And once they are proven effective, they must implement them!

IMPROVE TRAINING AND SUPPORT FOR TEACHERS

My fellow teachers and I attended a wide range of teacher training programs, from the Ivy League to lesser-known state colleges. Some, like me, had earned master's degrees before teaching; others were taking courses while teaching; still others went through summer boot camps like Teach For America. Yet we all had one thing in common: Almost no one thought the education courses we took were helpful or relevant. We weren't the only ones dissatisfied: An exhaustive 2013 study by the National Council on Teacher Quality labeled teacher training programs "an industry of mediocrity," finding that less than 10 percent of rated programs earned three stars or more out of four.

Our courses were often painfully theoretical and usually taught by people who had been in the classroom only for a short time or very long ago. As one coworker opined, "If I could have had even a fraction of those grad school hours back in sleep, I would have been a better teacher by far." A much greater percentage of coursework must be tied to real-world scenarios about how to actually teach and manage kids and must be taught by experts who have actually been in those settings.

Speaking of experts, all programs require their students to log a significant number of hours observing teachers in action, but this time is valuable only if those teachers are models worth emulating. Also, simply observing is not enough; teachers in training also need to watch videos of master teachers in action and hear why and how their approaches work.

GET TEACHERS UNIONS ON BOARD

The great majority of our nation's teachers are hardworking and competent, and they deserve strong unions to represent their interests. I appreciated many of the hard-won workplace protections and benefits the union afforded me, but I also saw the union protect incompetence and stifle change.

In the simplest terms, unions must be more willing to work with the administration so they can fire the least effective teachers; change lockstep compensation; reconsider evaluation, seniority, and tenure; and create incentives to put the best teachers in the neediest schools. We must reward and support the politicians on the left and the right who hold the feet of uncooperative unions to the fire.

Smart school districts and unions are working together on reform and avoiding the animosity that serves neither students, teachers, nor administrators. In Boston, for example, teachers in district- and union-supported "pilot schools" can vote to amend the union contract and expand the school day or year, establish higher achievement targets, and change their compensation structure. In New Haven, Connecticut, the union consented to a new evaluation system in 2010 where teachers set their own goals for student performance, which accounts for about half of their evaluation. The remainder of the evaluation is based on a review of the teacher's instructional methods. Underperforming teachers are given ample opportunity to improve. By 2013, the new system resulted in the removal of sixty-two teachers, while helping many others improve their performance.

For their cooperation, union members must be rewarded with better compensation. Not only is it logical that better wages will attract more qualified people to the field, but research bears it out. One study out of Stanford and UC Davis showed that increasing teachers' wages by 10 percent reduced the dropout rate by 3 to 4 percent.

INCREASE RESOURCES FOR THE MOST DISRUPTIVE AND THE MOST GIFTED STUDENTS

I remember how hopeful and excited I was when some of my most troubled and disruptive students were suspended from my classroom. *At last, I can teach and the kids will learn*, I thought. But in retrospect it always seemed like others would fill their shoes. What's more, the suspended students usually returned more resentful from being relegated to little more than a holding cell. These students need more resources, not warehousing. They should be given individual, group, and family therapy, offered behavioral change programs, and provided with out-of-school mentors. These students would also benefit from being assigned to the most veteran teachers and offered additional support in their classrooms.

Moreover, a new crop of "second-chance" high schools is showing promise in helping chronically unsuccessful kids. Instruction is personalized, classes are small, internships and work experience are offered, and, most important, every student is paired with an advocate / social worker who helps them deal with the life circumstances that usually landed them there in the first place. In most schools, counselors often have more than three hundred students in their caseloads; in these settings, it is usually limited to two dozen. I was encouraged to learn recently that one of my least focused and most nonacademic Union Street students had earned a prestigious Regents diploma and gained valuable work experience at a second-chance school in the Bronx.

Similarly, for the most able students, we must create more gifted and talented programs where they can move at an accelerated pace and compete with equally talented peers. (Sadly, there is no federal requirement that schools offer gifted services for students and few dollars allocated to states to provide them. As of 2013, fourteen states provided not one penny of funding for gifted education.)

The sooner and more intensively such programs are available for students at both ends of the achievement spectrum, the better. In a phenomenon known as the Matthew effect, new research shows that third graders who lack proficiency in reading are four times more likely to become high school dropouts than their peers. The movement toward quality, universal pre-K programs is key; New York City will be an important laboratory as it implements the policy in the coming years.

INNOVATE AND TEST!

It's time for more radical experiments and sensible innovations. There is little to lose. Fear of failure shouldn't hold us back, because we are already failing millions of students and teachers. For example, what if we tried paying good teachers what they're really worth? The Equity Project (TEP) Charter School in the academically underperforming Washington Heights neighborhood in New York City is doing just that. Teachers are paid a minimum of $125,000 a year, plus a potential $25,000 performance bonus, in exchange for their taking on roles that administrators play in other schools.

Why not tackle students' out-of-school challenges as forcefully as we try to remove in-school obstacles? Harlem Children's Zone is an ambitious attempt to do so for a hundred-block section of Harlem with a comprehensive array of services. There are many other smaller programs that partner with existing districts to provide outside services. Say Yes to Education, for example, offers tutoring, extended day programs, health and legal services, counseling, college guidance, and ultimately the promise of a college scholarship. Providence, Rhode Island, is piloting a program that encourages low-income parents to speak more words to their preschoolers to try to erase the yawning literacy gap that is already apparent by kindergarten.

What about bringing charter schools and traditional district schools into greater conversation with one another about their practices, successes, and failures? The 141-school network of KIPP charter schools serves mostly low-income students of color, who have a nationwide college graduation rate of around 8–9 percent. By contrast, 44 percent of students who completed eighth grade at KIPP ten or more years ago have now graduated from a four-year college. How can KIPP's success be scaled up to include more students and more schools? On the flip side, magnet schools in Hartford have been successful in bringing together a diverse array of students—from poor, inner-city neighborhoods and wealthy suburbs alike—and helping them all succeed. Other districts, as well as urban charter school networks that tend to segregate students by race and class, can learn from Hartford's approach.

However, all these systematic issues pale in front of the wellspring of all social problems:

END POVERTY, THE ROOT OF EDUCATIONAL FAILURE

When I saw firsthand the life circumstances of many of my students, my reaction was not "Why are so few showing up for school and failing so badly?" but rather, "How do so many have the wherewithal to show up at all?" As long as our society and our leadership expect the educational system to singlehandedly reverse the crippling legacy of long-term poverty, the system itself and attempts to reform it are doomed to failure. There are many proven steps we can take to improve education for the poor—there are even more untested ideas that we must try—but the real root of the problem is not the schools, it's poverty. If, like so many of my students, you faced serious poverty and its collateral damage on your family—unemployment, eviction, poor housing, incarceration, untreated physical and mental illness, deportation, and addiction—would you really feel it's important to fill out a work sheet on Egyptian hieroglyphics, to factor polynomials, or to delve into photosynthesis?

Poverty and its drag on education are not new, but it is about to become an even more serious problem because of a string of simple facts:

1. *The number of poor people in the United States is growing.* The number of Americans living in poverty has risen to an astounding 43.6 million people, the highest number since poverty rates were published in 1959. Twenty-two percent of our children are now living in poverty.

2. *The gap between rich and poor is growing.* American income inequality is currently at its highest point since the Great Depression.

3. *When there is an economic gap, there is an academic achievement gap.* The educational achievement gap between rich and poor children is nearly 40 percent larger for those born in 2001 than for those born in 1975. Countries with the greatest income disparity tend to have the greatest educational achievement gaps, and the United States leads the way in this dubious distinction.

These developments are serious economic, moral, and security threats to the nation. Even the most partisan elements of our two parties can agree on this, and yet the debate too often stays narrowly focused on schools as the sole solution.

But we can't tackle poverty if our leadership won't even discuss it. The Obama administration has said little and done less for the chronically poor, offering largely indirect measures like tax cuts for the working poor and focusing on the temporarily poor affected by the economic crisis. Our president, whose family was at one point on public assistance, has never made a major speech about poverty since taking the White House.

Eliminating poverty is a fantastic and expensive idea that lacks political will and widespread support, you say?

Not necessarily. In a compelling twist, many of the most effective steps we can take to alleviate poverty will not require higher taxes, and in some cases could even reduce them. Take, for example, passing living wage legislation, reforming immigration policy, or addressing the fact that we have the largest incarcerated population in the history of the world (the majority of whom are nonviolent). Other initiatives such as universal pre-K and broader health-care coverage would require more tax dollars, but there are compelling arguments that they would pay for themselves in relatively short order. And even if it does cost money, somehow we found the funds to spend $3 trillion on two recent wars of doubtful legitimacy and efficacy and last year racked up $60 billion in prison expenses.

Let me add a little international inspiration to the mix. Much has been written about Finland, widely considered to have one of the world's most successful and rigorous educational systems. It has been first among nations—or close to first—in several key global assessments including the vaunted PISA (Programme for International Student Assessment) test. Despite outspending nearly every other country in education, the United States is very much in the middle of the pack in PISA results. But what is less well known about Finland is that only sixty years ago it had a lackluster record in education. In post–World War II Finland, just 10 percent of students graduated from high school. With a concerted national will, thoughtful education policy, and a strong social safety net, they have risen to the top. South Korea, another leader in several key measures, has made a similar meteoric rise during roughly the same period of time. In short, nations can and have drastically changed their educational destinies in short order, and so can we. (It's worth noting that when you break down the PISA results, it's America's poverty that is bringing its results down: Higher-income American students and states score right near the top of the global heap.)

All this might sound like tired, lefty hippie talk, but it's true.

Simply put, the American Dream, the truest manifestation of a functioning democracy, has never been more at risk, and only the twin movements of poverty eradication and education reform will revive it.

If we are proactive, informed, and realistic, if we give up our childish hopes for silver bullets and quick fixes, if we move beyond lip service and really make these movements a central part of the national agenda, there is surely hope that we can achieve the full promise of our democracy.

I realize that all these things are infinitely easier said than done, but what endeavor is more worthy or critical? Every great social movement—abolition, suffrage, and the early civil rights movement—has seemed ludicrously unrealistic at its outset, but utterly inevitable at its attainment. We are the richest and most powerful nation on earth, and we can enlist some of the most gifted problem solvers in the world in the struggle. If we choose, we can create an ethical and effective educational system that can be our greatest and most lasting legacy.

It can, and it must, be done.

Acknowledgments

I have many people to thank for making this memoir a reality. Its creation was improbable, lengthy, and complicated.

Mindy Lewis was the loving midwife of its birth. She taught me when to push, how to breathe, and when to scream. Because of her, I walked into the Writer's Voice classroom at the West Side Y never having written a single word and walked out a published author.

Tricia Boczkowski has been a tireless champion of the book, even when it was little more than a random string of frantically told anecdotes on the beach on Fire Island. Her hand holding, advocacy, and keen eye at every step made the book possible. Similarly, Piper Kerman showed me how memoir writing is done and offered great encouragement all along the way.

I am endlessly grateful to my agent, Jim Levine, of Levine Greenberg Rostan Literary Agency, whose passionate interest in education led him to see the promise of this project where others only saw doubt. We were connected by the late Peter Workman, not only a giant in the field of publishing, but a true mensch.

My deepest thanks go to my editor at Grand Central Publishing, Emily Griffin, for her perpetual encouragement, patience, and tireless work on every aspect of this book. Throughout the process, she was true to her word that she is a writer's editor. I appreciate Jamie Raab's and Rick Wolff's willingness to take a risk on a first-time author, and Sonya Cheuse for her early advocacy.

I am grateful for the deep thinking of Professor Meira Levinson of the Harvard Graduate School of Education, who knocked quite a bit of sense into both my final chapter and me. I owe an enormous debt of gratitude to Andrew Solomon and James Ryan for being early and vocal champions of the project. Sheila Adams, Franchesca Diaz, James Ding, Leslie-Bernard Joseph, Dan-el Padilla Peralta, Milly Silva, and Jennifer Wynn were thoughtful readers and sources of inspiration from "Project Advance." My colleagues, in particular my terrifically supportive boss, were with me throughout this long journey and offered tremendous encouragement. My fellow students at the Writer's Voice served up the perfect blend of critique and reassurance at the early stages of the book. The gang at Above and Beyoncè were my tireless cheerleaders.

Each of these trusted and incisive readers prodded me to a better book: Adina Popescu Berk, David Boyer, Lisa Cashin, Doris Davis, Lou and Maggie DiFabio, Heidi Dorow, Rachel Ehrlich, Ivelys Figueroa, Doni Gewirtzman, Diana Y. Greiner, Sara Gurwitch, Holly Link, Glenn Mason, Lissa Perlman, Tashi Ridley, Larry Smith, David Suisman, David Thorpe, Nutty Trimarco, Julie Veltman, and Chandler Wells.

Other champions of the project include: Rose Arce, Susie Bartlett, Jake Bowers, April Salazar Froncek, Jeff Lee, Robert Levy, Arlene Malave-Vazquez, Christoph Marshall, Lisa Martin, Alberto Orso, Francesca Ryan, Erin Shigaki, Sherry Susiman, Ellen Umansky, and Rhonda Zapatka.

I appreciate the students, teachers, and staff from my time teaching for lending me their lives, stories, and voices in the hope of bringing greater awareness to the state of education and the American underclass today, particularly my students J. and S. To my own teachers, stretching from first grade with Sister Concepta to college with Dr. Irma Jaffe, I am indebted.

To my loving family—both immediate and extended, including the Alexanders, Attis, Kantors, Herbies, and Zalutskys—whose genes crackle with storytelling DNA, thank you. My parents, Julie and Dave, have been behind me every step of the way, and my sisters have it made their lives' work to help the disenfranchised; they deserve far more credit than I do. And finally, to Sam, to whom this book is dedicated, for just about everything.

About the Author

ED BOLAND has dedicated his entire professional life to nonprofit causes as a fundraiser and communications expert. He has worked predominantly for educational institutions, but also for arts and social service organizations. Boland was an admissions officer at his alma mater, Fordham, and later at Yale, and taught in China as a Princeton in Asia fellow. An avid volleyball player and cook, he lives in New York with his husband, filmmaker Sam Zalutsky.